The Invent To Learn Guide to 3D Printing in the Classroom: Recipes for Success

The Invent To Learn Guide to 3D Printing in the Classroom: Recipes for Success

David D. Thornburg, PhD
Norma Thornburg, MA
Sara Armstrong, PhD

Constructing Modern Knowledge Press

Constructing Modern Knowledge Press

www.cmkpress.com

EDU039000 EDUCATION / Computers & Technology

EDU029030 EDUCATION / Teaching Methods & Materials / Science & Technology

ISBN: 978-0-9891511-4-6

Cover design: Yvonne Martinez

"We are all designers now. We may as well get good at it."

— *Chris Anderson*

Author of 'Makers: The New Industrial Revolution'

Contents

On Your Own

Foreword

3D printers are hot. They're so hot that even schools are buying them. Although, schools are thought to be late adopters of emerging technology, I've been pleasantly surprised by how many already own 3D printers.

Investing in a school's first 3D printer may be a down payment on the future of education; a future in which learning to learn with one's head, heart, and hands will be equally critical. Making things is a great way to learn and an ability to make the things you need is an important 21st Century skill. The confidence and competence required to solve problems that the school curriculum or your teachers never anticipated will be the mark of a life well lived.

That said, once a school gets their 3D printer working reliably enough for each seventh grader to print an identical Yoda keychain, many educators are at a loss for next steps. That's where this book comes in. David, Norma, and Sara share 18 projects designed to help teachers teach 3D design and enrich multiple curricular subjects.

Once you get the hang of 3D printing, you will realize how simple the hardware is. The real revolution may not be the printer as much as it is the democratization of design and the Z-axis.

For decades, CAD/CAM (computer-aided design/computer-aided manufacturing) software was too complicated and expensive for more than a few students to use. It was relegated to drafting classes and vocational settings. Now affordable and accessible software like Tinkercad make design child's play. The ease of use associated with this new generation software does not mean that the design process has become any less rigorous. Design is where the mathematical reasoning, artistic sensibility, and engineering processes come to the fore.

We were all taught about the X- and Y-axes in school math class. Some of us may even use that coordinate system from time-to-time. However, with the exception of the occasional SAT question about the volume of a cylinder, you might conclude that we live in a 2D world. 3D printing and its design software bring us the Z-axis and provide an authentic context for using and understanding three-dimensional space. This book makes the conscious pedagogical decision to transition from 2D design to 3D artifact.

A common trope in educational discussions is, "Technology changes constantly." Oh, if only that were true. If your school has spent two decades teaching kids to make PowerPoint presentations on subjects they don't care about for an audience that doesn't exist, then "technology" hasn't changed much for you or your students (in school) since *Alf* went off the air.

In rare instances, there *are* revolutionary advances in technology that impact classroom practice. The technologies most closely associated with the maker movement, including: 3D printers and laser cutters, open-source microcontrollers like Arduino, and new ways to embed circuitry in everyday objects may indeed represent a paradigm shift in educational technology.

Since affordable and accessible 3D design is in its infancy, the authors provide you with experience exploring a variety of different software environments. You will also need to adapt instructions for the proclivities of your specific printer. Through this experience, you should be able to decide which software best meets the needs of you and your students. The hardware and software *will* change. Some of the companies producing your favorite software or printer may not last a school year. As a pioneer, you will need to remain flexible and on the lookout for better solutions. Once you find a software solution (or two) that works for you, use it. You don't need to jump on every bandwagon or pretend that your students are learning something valuable because you keep changing software. Understanding which tools you choose to use and why is important.

In 1985, I flew cross-country to attend one of my first educational computing conferences. At the opening reception, I stumbled upon two gentlemen engaged in a mind-blowing discussion of Ada Lovelace's work. One of the combatants was Brian Silverman and the other, David Thornburg. Over the past four decades, Brian and David have contributed as much as anyone in the world to what children are able to do with computers.

As I eavesdropped on the fascinating conversation, I silently vowed to spend the rest of my life in the company of smart people like the Lady Ada fans at that party. Fortunately for me, both men have become great friends and close colleagues. Prior to meeting David, I was familiar with his work through his many articles and the fantastic Logo books he authored. I had also taught with the Koala Pad, an affordable and reliable drawing tablet he had designed. David was already an accomplished mathematician, computer scientist, engineer, and designer with Xerox PARC and Stanford on his CV by the time I met him. Since then, David has been a great friend, collaborator, and trusted advisor.

David Thornburg has a knack for anticipating hot trends and getting educators excited about the future just around the corner. His presentations and countless books have inspired two genera-tions of teachers to use technology in a playful, deep, and constructive fashion.

3D printing and David fit each other like a hand and virtual reality glove. David is a renaissance man – part mathematician, part computer scientist, part engineer, part educator, part designer, part musician, part humorist, and full-time tinkerer.

My longtime colleagues in the Thornburg Center, Norma Thornburg and Sara Armstrong joined David in bringing this volume to life. They too have made indelible contributions to the field of education.

It seemed natural that Constructing Modern Knowledge Press would publish a book by David, Norma and Sara, which situates the 3D printing revolution in a classroom context. I commend you, brave pioneer, as you and your students design the future together.

— Gary Stager, PhD

Publisher, Constructing Modern Knowledge Press

Acknowledgements

The authors want to thank their supporters in this project – John Westrum, Gary Carnow, Glenn Bull, Sylvia Martinez, Gary Stager, Jenny Wojcik, and, especially, those teachers who tried out many of the projects in this book, helping us to make it even better than it would have been!

About this book

This book represents the most up-to-date information we have on 3D printers, software, and their use in schools. This is a fast-growing field, and things are changing rapidly. We know that as time goes on, technology will advance, prices will change, new products will appear, and URLs will break.

Links

To save space and knowing that you cannot click on a book, we have shortened some long URLs using the Google link shortening service, which will redirect you to the actual URL. For your convenience, all URLs, books, and resources mentioned in this book can be found on the resource page of the InventToLearn3D.com website.

Getting Started

Introduction

Until now, our personal computers were only capable of creating artifacts that lived on paper or the screen – text, animation, graphics, websites. Commercial factories have been able to "print" actual objects, but those printers were hugely expensive and the design software was extremely complex. 3D printers have finally become affordable, portable, and easy-to-use. New software allows anyone, including children, to design 3D objects. Models can be built by sending a 3D art file to a special printer that then builds the part from many materials, depending on the need. These materials have typically included plastic, metal, and ceramics, but those are not the only materials appropriate for this technology. Now the fabrication materials used range from cement to living cells. Here are a few applications that already exist, and we can only imagine how others will develop in the future.

Rapid prototyping

Industrial strength 3D printers are still pretty expensive. While they make sense for large companies to purchase, there are other options that provide the service of building parts from the designer's file. As this is being written, some UPS stores are offering walk-in service for people who need high quality plastic prototypes built. Other companies such as Shapeways (www.shapeways.com), provide a wide range of services for professionals and amateurs alike. You can even sell your finished parts through them if you like, and your models are not limited to plastic.

Customized parts

Sculptors like Bathsheba Grossman (www.bathsheba.com) use 3D printing in a variety of materials to make jewelry and other sculptures, mostly based on complex mathematical models (she has degrees both in mathematics and fine arts). She also does commissioned work, sometimes making very large pieces that are on display in various parts of the world.

At the other extreme, you might find yourself needing to repair a broken cabinet latch by making a new one yourself. This kind of custom work is tailor-made for 3D printers.

Home construction

Using a technology developed at the University of Southern California called Contour Crafting, it is possible to build a 2,000 square foot house in 24 hours using a 3D printer that works with cement. As the house is being built, openings are left in the walls for plumbing and electrical services. Caterpillar is one of the companies that has expressed an interest in this technology.

Medicine

3D printing is perfect for the fabrication of parts used in prosthetic limbs since the shapes can be easily customized for each person who needs them. For example, Leon McCarthy was born without fingers on his left hand. Paul McCarthy, Leon's father, realized that the high price meant a factory-made device wasn't an option, so he borrowed a 3D printer from his son's school and printed his son a hand. It works great – and if parts break, they are easy to build again (goo.gl/Lfu4eC).

But prosthetic limbs are just the start. Dr. Anthony Atala is working on a process for 3D printing new human kidneys using materials grown from the patient's own cells (so there is no rejection). In the TED video on his work (goo.gl/U24DJ), Dr. Atala describes a process that, while not yet approved, may someday solve the problem of treating the tremendous number of people who suffer from kidney failure.

For those with heart problems, John Rogers from the University of Illinois at Urbana-Champaign used a 3D printer to create an anatomically accurate reproduction of a rabbit heart. Once he had the heart template, he embedded tiny instruments in a silicon membrane designed to fit snugly over the heart. The end result is a form-fitting silicon sheath that keeps sensors in place, yet remains flexible enough to not interfere with cardiac pumping. While it will be years before such a device will be available for human hearts, it is a project worth watching!

Space

A 3D-printed rocket engine was tested last year by a chapter of the Students for the Exploration and Development of Space (SEDS) at the University of California, San Diego, which spent the last eight months developing the metal rocket engine, named Tri-D.

Private groups and NASA have been exploring how to use additive manufacturing. The Tri-D engine was printed from a cobalt chromium alloy using a technique known as direct metal laser sintering (DMLS). This approach saves both time and money and allows different designs to be built and tested quite rapidly, compared with the time and expense of building a rocket engine in traditional ways.

Spare parts in space

What spare parts are needed in the International Space Station (ISS)? The fact is, we don't know, and the cost of shipping parts from Earth is fairly high. But, if the ISS had a 3D printer, people on board could make many of their own replacement parts as needed. Of course this requires a 3D printer that works in a microgravity environment. A company, Made in Space (www.madeinspace.us), has developed a printer that is scheduled to be delivered to the ISS in August 2014. 3D printing is, literally, out of this world.

Many more examples and intriguing applications can be found at the 3ders website: (www.3ders.org).

At this point you might be thinking that this is all great stuff, but wonder what, if anything, any of this has to do with education.

The Goal of This Book

There is no question in our minds that 3D printers are powerful tools in the classroom. These devices are getting less expensive every year, and many schools are already finding ways to incorporate them in the teaching of science and engineering. Students can start with 3D drawings done with a variety of programs that export STL (stereolithography) files. But the printing of objects, by itself, does nothing to advance education. The real value comes from students engaging in the design process and experimenting with the objects they create. With this in mind, it is easy to see how these devices can be used in a wide variety of subjects – especially science, technology, mathematics, and engineering (STEM), but also in the arts, humanities, languages, and social studies.

This book includes some sample projects that touch on several curricular areas, and cut across multiple grade levels. For example, the process of designing and building a tangram set incorporates a lot of mathematics, and this is even before students work with the finished tangram set itself. A project like the design of a propeller-driven car involves many design issues that influence car performance, and the experimentation in the design of this vehicle incorporates lots of physics. We've provided information in each project showing its connection to the new Next Generation Science Standards (NGSS). Some projects also list connections to the Common Core State Standards for mathematics. The central idea in NGSS is that students develop understanding, not just memorize content. By designing, making, and working with tangible projects, the development of understanding is enhanced far beyond what is possible in the traditional book- and lecture-based classroom.

While any of the projects we explore can be created with a powerful 3D design program like SketchUp and others we will describe, it is easier to start with a powerful 2D drawing tool like Inkscape, and then to extrude (add height to) the finished drawing into a three-dimensional shape. The advantage of starting with traditional 2D drawing tools is that students and teachers are already familiar with them. While there are many useful shapes that can't be made this way, there is enough to be done with extruded 2D shapes to build the ability to design in three dimensions, leading to more skills with the use of other programs that work directly in the 3D design space.

Our projects are designed to be built on inexpensive hobbyist 3D printers that typically cost less than $4,000. All projects in this book were built using the Afinia H-Series printer (www.afinia.com), but they can all be made on any plastic extrusion printer you might have.

A note about this book

This book contains projects as a set of step-by-step recipes written in a way that lets you make progress with little to no previous experience with the software. Once you get comfortable with the tools we are using, you won't need such detailed instructions. However, until then, we hope you find the step-by-step approach helpful. Each project is self-contained and does not require completion of a previous activity. Therefore, some instructions are repeated in multiple projects.

Why recipes?

To be perfectly honest, we are not huge fans of recipes. In an ideal setting, we'd like students and teachers to design and build creations of their own, learning through tinkering. The tinkering process is important for several reasons. First, it sometimes leads to unexpected results, and sometimes things don't go as planned. In both of these cases, the opportunities for learning are magnified.

A hybrid approach where students are given a general task and then left free to create their own designs germane to the task is the goal. Our experience with 3D printers and design software is that there is a steep learning curve made trickier by occasional hardware idiosyncrasies. Once students get comfortable with the tools, they will be busily designing amazing things we never imagined!

Opportunities and Challenges of 3D Printing in Education

Educators have good questions about 3D printing in the classroom. It's not enough to say that a technology is "new" and "cool" (even though it is). This chapter answers commonly-asked questions, outlines the opportunities, and explores some of the more commonly expressed concerns about 3D printing in schools.

Challenges

3D printers are expensive

They used to be very expensive, but their prices are dropping every year. The printer we use costs about $1500, but there are other good looking ones in the $700 price range. The real question is what opportunity is lost if we don't get tools like this in front of our students?

Danger from hot parts

The print nozzle gets very hot – about 260 Celsius. This is why there are usually shrouds surrounding this part so fingers can't get in the way! The heated plate on some printers is kept at about the boiling point of water, so you want to be sure you are wearing gloves if you need to touch it while it is still hot. Of course, anyone who has used a glue gun or an oven knows that there are hot parts that we need to avoid touching.

Fumes from the melting plastic

Both glue guns and 3D printers emit a small amount of fumes from the melted plastic. We haven't seen that this poses any health concerns, so if you use your printer in a well-ventilated place, fumes are not a problem.

Kids can hurt themselves removing parts from the printer base

Unlike paper printers that eject pages automatically, 3D parts typically have to be removed from the printing surface by hand. This takes some care, and students need to be shown how to handle the separation tool so they don't get cut. Students also need to wear good leather gloves when working with sharp tools to avoid accidental cuts. Even so, it never hurts to have a few adhesive bandages available for minor cuts. The general rule is, ten fingers in, ten fingers out, and safety standards have to be established by the teacher.

Takes time from other "real learning" activities

While the design part of 3D printing takes classroom time, the actual printing can be done in the background, and even overnight if needed. The point is that, used effectively, 3D printing can be connected to many curricular areas and provides one more way to engage students with their learning.

Kids can make guns

While this is technically true, that is not going to be a problem for printers used in the classroom under your supervision. Second, the gun designs we've seen are as likely to blow up in someone's hand as they are to shoot a bullet. We honestly don't see this as a concern.

Kids can waste time just downloading items from Thingiverse and printing them

Thingiverse and Youmagine are wonderful sites with lots of cool things to download and print. But the real value comes from moving beyond this to designing your own parts. David's father always said that firewood warms you twice – once when you cut it, and again when you burn it. A similar idea holds true for 3D designs. This book suggests the design process itself is just as important as working with whatever has been made.

What about violating copyright?

That's the great thing about the Maker Movement. Just about everyone wants to share their designs with everyone else, and loves to get comments and learn about variations from those who try them. Check on any design you want to download, and you will usually find a Creative Commons license for Attribution (you can use, tweak, and share as long as you credit the creator), which may include other gentle restrictions, such as Non-commercial or Share Alike. When your students build their own creations, they may well want to make them available to others under Creative Commons licensing. (See Creative Commons for more information about licensing: www.creativecommons.org).

Why should young children use 3D printers?

Engineering is part of the Next Generation Science Standards for K–12, and 3D printing helps develop the kinds of skills that develop good design practices – practices that are essential to engineering. Also, kids of all ages love seeing something they have made, no matter how simple it is. Finished projects can be taken home and are likely to be treasured for a long time.

Opportunities

3D parts are tangible

We have a generation of children brought up in a virtual world where objects are shown as displays on screens, not in tangible form. Many years ago, MIT's Nicholas Negroponte said, "Bits are the new atoms." With the rise of 3D printing in schools, we can now say that atoms are the new bits! 3D printers can be used for many things, including the construction of math manipulatives of your own design.

3D parts are personal expressions

Physical objects students make in school are likely to become treasured possessions for years to come. This has always been true. Years ago, when Norma's daughter, Luciana, attended Kendall College majoring in culinary arts, she built a small piano completely out of chocolate. Even though this artifact was made many years ago, it still is on display at home (and is holding up pretty well!).

3D parts can be used in other projects

Another area of engineering exploration for kids is robotics – computer-controlled machines that perform a specific task. In the process of designing a robotic model, students may need gears and other specialized parts they can design and make on a 3D printer. This is a completely different approach to robotic structures than those based on LEGO blocks. Finished robots that students make can even be taken home when the project is over.

A Word About Standards

At the time of this book's publication, the Next Generation Science Standards (NGSS) and Common Core State Standards (CCSS) are receiving a lot of attention. Many of the projects in this book support those standards.

Let's start with the Common Core Math Standards – there are only eight of them:

1. Make sense of problems and persevere in solving them.
2. Reason abstractly and quantitatively.
3. Construct viable arguments and critique the reasoning of others.
4. Model with mathematics.
5. Use appropriate tools strategically.
6. Attend to precision.
7. Look for and make use of structure.
8. Look for and express regularity in repeated reasoning.

Looking at these standards in the context of 3D printing, several of them leap out. Virtually all the projects in this book call for accuracy in measurements (Standard 2). Modeling with mathematics (Standard 4) is also commonplace, as is the strategic use of appropriate tools (Standard 5). Precision (Standard 6) is important when structures are made of parts that have to fit together. The use of structure in designs relates quite well to Standard 7. By challenging themselves in designing objects for the 3D printer, students will certainly participate in problem solving and persevering until the object is made to their satisfaction (Standard 1).

In other words, virtually every design students make and print incorporates six of the eight math standards. Several of the projects in this book connect to the remaining standards, and these connections will be made for each relevant project.

As for the NGSS, there are seven core principles that define the scope of these standards. In exploring the scope, we share our comments on how this book (and 3D printing in general) connects to the standards:

1. K–12 Science Education should reflect the interconnected nature of science as it is practiced and experienced in the real world.
2. The Next Generation Science Standards are student performance expectations – NOT curriculum.
3. The Science Concepts in the NGSS build coherently from K–12.

4. The NGSS focus on deeper understanding of content as well as application of content.

5. Science and Engineering are integrated in the NGSS, from K–12.

6. The NGSS are designed to prepare students for college, career, and citizenship.

7. The NGSS and Common Core State Standards (English Language Arts and Mathematics) are aligned.

All seven of these characteristics of the NGSS apply to 3D printing in the way we are presenting it.

As for the standards themselves, the NGSS is divided into four disciplinary core ideas: Physical Science, Life Science, Earth and Space Science, and Engineering. While all our projects connect to Engineering, some of them connect as well to other core ideas, especially Physics and Life Sciences.

How Consumer 3D Printers Work

The kinds of 3D printers likely to be found in schools are basically similar to glue guns with some motors attached. OK, that is a bit of an overstatement, but if you know how a glue gun works, you are well on your way to knowing how your 3D printer works. A plastic material is heated up and squished through a small hole to create a thin line of plastic. If the "glue gun" is connected to motors that move the print nozzle left and right, forward and back, and up and down, this process can be used to create very complex parts following directions provided to the printer by a computer. (By the way, if you want to build your own 3D printer from a real glue gun, there are some instructions here (goo.gl/zUleZ), but we don't recommend that approach.)

Of course 3D printers don't use glue sticks, they use plastic filament generally made from one of two thermoplastics: ABS (acrylonitrile butadiene styrene) or PLA (polyactic acid). The filament (which usually starts out about 1.75 mm in thickness) is heated to soften it enough to be pushed through a nozzle onto a surface called a build plate to make a line about 0.15 mm thick. This is about the thickness of a human hair. The printer lays down many of these thin lines of plastic to make one layer. Then the print nozzle moves up a tiny bit and another layer of thin lines is printed. As the layers of plastic are built up one by one, they combine to create a three-dimensional object.

The choice of plastic you use is based on several factors. ABS is a plastic made from petroleum and PLA is made from natural starch. ABS shrinks a bit on cooling, making it important to have a heated platform when building a part. Based on these characteristics, you might think PLA is the obvious choice. The problem with PLA is that it is brittle, and ABS is much stronger. Parts that get a lot of use should probably be made with ABS.

Both materials are potentially recyclable, but you must send ABS material to special recycling companies, and while PLA is organic and theoretically compostable, you must use a specific time-consuming composting process. Neither PLA nor ABS can be tossed in the recycling bins.

Because each of these plastics has a different softening temperature, the printer needs to be set up for one kind of plastic at a time. Some printers are designed to handle both kinds, and some are designed to use just one kind – typically PLA. In either case, the filament usually comes on a spool holding about a kilogram of material and is available in a wide range of colors.

What size parts can I build?

This depends on the printer you have chosen. Many printers allow the fabrication of objects that can be put in a box 12 cm on a side, or about the size of a cupcake, and some work with even larger spaces than this.

How long does it take to build something?

The volume of the part is a critical factor. Because parts are built layer by layer, a finished part may have several hundred layers, each of which is 0.15 mm in thickness. While small parts can be built in a half-hour, large parts may need to be built overnight.

What factors should I look for when purchasing a school 3D printer?

The process of choosing a printer can be a bit intimidating. There are lots of printers on the market and it seems like new ones are coming out every week. And, if that were not enough, some vendors make several models. One good place to start looking is the MAKE Magazine annual guide to 3D printing (goo.gl/kqVWjU). The approach taken in their reviews is to set up a large number of different printers and make the same objects for side-by-side comparison. The only problem with their review process is that they obviously can't include any new printers entering the market after their review is published.

That said, there are some factors you can consider when choosing a 3D printer for educational use. Based on these factors you can then visit the website of the printer manufacturer to see how well they meet your needs. Unlike the world of personal computing where the market is filled with well-known brands, the 3D printer world has lots of new entrants, so brand name is less likely to play a significant role.

- **Type** – The two choices for inexpensive printers are those that use extruded plastic filaments (fused filament fabrication), and those that use laser beams to harden a liquid resin. The majority use fused filaments, which gives you a wide range of color choices for the final part, as well as two types of plastic depending on your needs. The liquid resin printers produce beautiful parts, but are more limited in colors. Also, the laser beam used to harden the plastic is probably not the best thing to have flashing around when children are present, even though the housing is made with a tinted plastic designed to block the laser light.

- **Price** – Prices range from $500 to about $2,000 for a good printer. While it is always true to some extent that you get what you pay for, there are some interesting printers being introduced with low price points. Assuming you have an adequate budget, we wouldn't let price be the driving factor in making a choice.

- **Out-of-the-box experience** – Some printers are a dream to set up: just pop them out of the box, load the filament, install some software, and start printing. Others require a bit of adjusting and calibration to use, but once this is done, everything is locked in place and you are ready to go.

- **Flexibility** – The two commonly-used plastics for 3D printers are ABS (acrylonitrile buta-diene styrene) and PLA (polyactic acid). Some printers can use both kinds of plastic, while others are set up for only one. Since the softening temperature for each of these is different, you need always to use the recommended plastic for a machine that only uses one type. Each of these plastics has about the same price, but they differ in a few ways. ABS is great for structural parts, but shrinks a little bit, making a heated bed (see below) a very good idea. Both plastics produce a slight odor when heated and pushed through the nozzle, so good ventilation is a great idea. ABS is recyclable, and PLA is biodegradable (it is made from either corn starch, tapioca roots, or sugar cane, depending on where in the world it is made).

- **Exposed wires** – Some 3D printers have wiring that can be seen when the printer is used. While these wires are insulated and safe to touch, you need to decide if this is an important factor in choosing your printer. Other printer designs are completely enclosed, hiding wires and other parts away from prying fingers. You may decide to get a printer where the kids can see everything in action while it is working, and just caution them to keep fingers away from the printer while it is running.

- **Exposed nozzle** – The extrusion nozzle is where the filament is heated and pushed through to make a very fine layer for the part being made. This nozzle typically is heated to around 260 C, pretty hot to the touch! While printers are usually covered with danger signs cautioning against touching heated areas of the printer when it is working, some printer designs make it easier for curious fingers to get where they shouldn't be. As long as kids are cautioned to keep their hands out of the printer while it is working, you should be OK.

- **Heated bed** – The bed on which the parts are being built can sometimes be heated to 100 C to keep the corners of large parts from peeling up during printing. When ABS is used, a heated bed is a very good idea. With PLA, while a nice option, a heated bed is not as critical.

- **Self-leveling platform** – The height between the platform and the nozzle needs to stay the same over the base area of the printed object. Otherwise the nozzle may run into the plate (potentially damaging the printer), or move too far away (producing plastic extrusions that harden before reaching the platform). Many printers have manual adjustment screws that let you level the plate by hand. This process is not terribly hard, but is inconvenient. For this reason, many of the newer model printers have self-leveling platforms. Personally, we think this is a great feature for printers used in schools.

- **Self-adjusting nozzle height** – Once the platform is leveled, the nozzle height has to be set just right. If it is too close to the platform, the nozzle may get plugged, keeping plastic from being added to the part. If it is too far away, the extruded plastic hardens before hitting the platform, thus ruining the part being built. Manual nozzle adjustment is fairly simple, but, as with self-leveling platforms, the option to automatically adjust nozzle height is also available on some printers.

- **Printing bed surface** – This is a topic of great interest. Some printers come with glass platforms, others with metal platforms, and other materials (e.g., fiberglass reinforced epoxy perf board) are commonplace. Except for the perf board, the platform typically needs to be coated with a material that has two features: It keeps the part from peeling and slipping during printing, and it makes it easy to remove the final part when it has been completed. There are lots of options that have been used and you will probably find a solution that works best for you. For example, a spritz of hairspray on a glass plate is one recommendation. Just don't cover the whole plate with spray. Another popular solution is the use of 3M blue painter's tape. Just be sure you don't get grease from your fingers on the tape when sticking it on the platform. Some like to use the purple Elmers washable school glue stick. A more elaborate system is to dissolve a little ABS in acetone and paint that on the platform before printing. This is probably not the best solution for school use because of the acetone.

Another surface that seems to work well for many people is Kapton tape. This costs a lot more that painter's tape, but it can often be used to make several parts before needing to be replaced. One of the more recent printing surface treatments is called BuildTak (www. buildtak.com). This surface is held to the build plate and works great for raftless printing with both ABS and PLA. One treatment lasts for a dozen print jobs or more, and it can easily be removed and replaced.

- **Raft vs. raftless printing** – Most printers give you the option to print your parts with or without a support raft. The raft is printed over a larger area than the part to help hold everything down. The problem is that, when you are done, you need to peel the raft off the part, typically with a sharp blade from a painter's spatula. If students have to remove a raft from their parts, be sure they are wearing leather gloves and holding the spatula so the cut is made away from them. While raftless printing solves this problem, there may still be support structures added to the part that have to be peeled away. Many times, this can be done by hand, or with an X-acto knife. Personally, we'd try raftless printing first, but many parts we make have been fabricated with rafts. One last point: No matter what, you will have lots of small plastic scraps coming from your parts. These should be put in a container for recycling (ABS) or biodegradable trash (PLA).

How much does filament cost and are there different choices?

Most filament is sold in 1 kg spools with a wide variety of color choices including glow-in-the-dark and metallic-looking options. You can also purchase different quality filament. This may be useful to print draft or prototype projects, switching to higher quality for finished projects. Filament comes in 1.75 mm and 3 mm sizes, but most inexpensive hobbyist 3D printers use 1.75 mm filament. At this time, filament costs around $30 – $50 per spool.

How much does it cost to print an average object?

One spool of filament can print hundreds of objects. The cost will vary depending on the weight of the object, which will be shown in the design software when you are ready to print. You can then calculate the cost by multiplying the weight of the object by the cost/kg of your filament.

How many objects can I print from one roll of filament?

Again, this will depend on the weight of your objects and how many you print during a given time period.

Can I print objects with multiple colors?

At this time, 3D printers that print multiple colors are more expensive than ones that print single-color objects. It is possible to carefully switch filament in the middle of a print, or of course, if your object has several parts, you can use different filament for each part. Other than that, most school 3D printers are printing single color objects. This will probably change in a few years!

What else do I need to purchase?

Several tools will be useful when you begin using your 3D printer. Always obey good safety practices and wear protective eyewear and gloves when using sharp tools. Consider starting with these:

- **Scraping tools** – When your printed object is finished, it will be attached to the build plate of the printer and will need to be removed. Sometimes this can take some scraping. Chisels and putty knives are useful for this.

- **Extra build plates** – Purchase several build plates so that a build plate can be removed with the object still attached, and then you can use a different build plate to start a new build.

- **Cleaning tools** – When you start to design more complex objects, your printer will add support structures for any overhanging material. This support material is flimsy and should break off easily, but may leave "nubs" or be in hard to reach places. Collect different types of metal picks and scrapers to find what works best for you and your students. Dental tools, ceramics and art tools, or jewelry-making tools may be useful.

- **Measuring tools** – Have different kinds of measuring tools available for students, including rulers, calipers, and others. As students gain experience, they should be able to create designs with more precision, for example, making parts that fit together snugly.

Other tips

Your printer manufacturer will have other suggestions for successful use of the printer. Look for educators online using the same printer to share ideas and suggestions. There are support forums and Google groups for many of the printer manufacturers and software as well. There are websites and videos showing tips for 3D printing, for example how to remove rafts, how to make the prints stick to the build plate (but not stick too much), etc.

Surface cleaning and smoothing

Because the 3D printed objects are made from very thin layers of plastic, the surface can look a bit rough. There is a great way to solve this problem. Take a new empty one-gallon paint can, put a few layers of paper towels on the inside walls with magnets to hold them in place, soak the towels with acetone, put your parts in the bottom of the can, loosely cover the can. After an hour or so, your parts will be shiny and smooth! Of course, you will want to do this in a well-ventilated area far away from flames, and use all necessary safety precautions.

How Do Students Create Designs?

3D designs can come from various sources. For example, the Thingiverse website (www.thingiverse.com) has thousands of designs created by people all over the world. Another similar site is Youmagine (www.youmagine.com). Designs can be freely downloaded and printed as they are posted. Alternatively, you can download a design and modify it to meet your particular needs using 3D modeling software.

The other extreme is to start with a blank screen in your 3D design software and create parts from scratch. Because 3D design software has a learning curve, it takes time to learn how to design things you might want to print. That said, the tinkering process is tremendously valuable, and is a goal worth working towards. In this book we suggest both the projects and the process of design (hence the title, Recipes for Success) with the goal that, as people get more comfortable with the tools, they will make the transition to designing things on their own.

There is a third path to design. In the past, you might have molded a prototype with modeling clay. Now you can use a 3D scanner to copy a 3D object so it may be reproduced on a 3D printer. Rather than just reproducing existing objects, you may use scans of existing objects as a base for sculpting and printing your own 3D object. Low resolution 3D scanners currently cost around $800, but there are ways you can build your own! The Instructables website has a few (for example: www.instructables.com/id/EASY-Kinect-3D-Scanner) that are inexpensive and a good way to get started. It is also possible to build a 3D image from a series of photos taken with a digital camera, and we will explore that in the next chapter.

No matter how you start, you will still need software to create and modify images of your 3D parts. These software programs are called Computer Aided Design (CAD) programs. The images you design are ultimately saved in an STL (STereoLithography) format file. The software that drives your printer takes an STL file and converts it to layers so it can be printed. No matter what printer you use, STL files are the starting place.

So, what software do you need? There are many superb high-end design programs you can buy, but there are a lot of free tools you can use as well. Our focus will be on the free tools.

The rest of this chapter introduces a few free titles that should be on your list.

> **Note:** The images in this chapter are designed to show you the overall look of the software screen, so don't worry about the details. In the project recipes, you will see detailed images of the icons and screen text of important project steps.

Inkscape

Mac, Windows, Linux

www.inkscape.org

Inkscape is primarily a drawing program for two-dimensional designs. It is an amazingly powerful tool that even automates the process of drawing complex objects like gears. Drawings created in Inkscape can be saved in the SVG (scalable vector graphic) format so they look great at any magnification. You can also export images in traditional graphics formats like PNG (portable network graphic) for websites, word processing documents, or presentations.

But the real power of Inkscape as a 3D drawing tool comes when you add height to your drawing, instantly turning 2D into 3D. To do this, install the support plug-in for 3D extrusion. The PathstoOpenSCAD extension for Inkscape and all instructions can be found at www.thingiverse.com/thing:25036

Select the part of the drawing you want to add height to, or extrude into a three-dimensional shape. Choose the extrusion option, and indicate how many millimeters you want the extrusion to be. A 3D OpenSCAD file is generated automatically. To get this shape to your printer, the next step is to open it in OpenSCAD, compile the image, and save it as an STL file. This sounds laborious, but it is easy to get the hang of it, and the whole process goes very quickly.

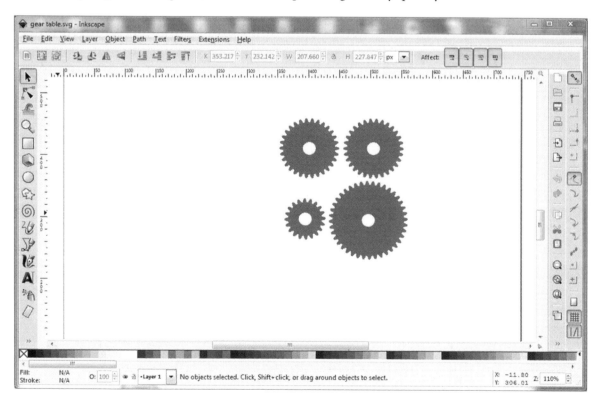

You may be wondering why we would recommend a two-dimensional drawing tool in the context of 3D printing. The reason is that, while building 3D objects on the computer screen is likely a new task to students, they probably use two-dimensional art programs all the time. Some students may be intimidated by starting with 3D designs, so our goal is to build from this strength on the path to (later) creating designs with purely 3D drawing tools.

Starting with 2D drawing also simplifies using measurement tools to create precise designs. We want students to understand how to design for precision, not just to "mess around." Beginning with 2D starts these good habits early.

> **Note:** Follow the installation directions for Inkscape very carefully, especially the Macintosh version, which requires the installation of an additional software application.

OpenSCAD

Mac, Windows, Linux

www.openscad.org

While we will largely use OpenSCAD as an extrusion tool for Inkscape, it is, in fact, a full 3D modeling tool that builds models from text commands. It has its own programming language that might be appropriate for high-schoolers to play with. An advantage of building geometric models in OpenSCAD is that they can be "parameterized" – expressed in a way that lets one design make several related shapes by changing the values of a few variables. For example, a propeller can be designed in OpenSCAD in a way that lets the end user change the number and size of the blades. This is a very useful feature, and quite a few Thingiverse models include OpenSCAD files for just that reason. Used in this way, students can tinker with existing models to create a custom part for their construction. The final model is displayed on the screen to be sure it is what you want before saving it as an STL file.

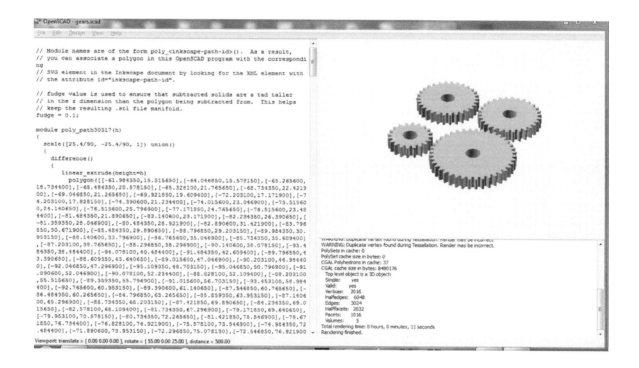

SketchUp Make

Mac, Windows

www.sketchup.com

SketchUp is a professional 3D modeling tool that is very good for creating geometric structures from scratch (architectural designs, for example). The free version (SketchUp Make) has all the features that students might need to build models of the parts they want to print. If your model can be built from boxes, cylinders, and balls, it is a great tool. It is not what we would choose for more organic shapes, though. The SketchUp Extension Warehouse has a free plug-in that lets you export your finished part as an STL file directly. Our only caution about this tool is that it is not the best program for editing completed STL files. They show up as a mass of dots and triangles, and we haven't found a way to render the surfaces as nicely as you can from models made in SketchUp in the first place. This is a shame, because older versions of SketchUp handled imported STL files much better. The good news is that there are many other alternatives for you to use.

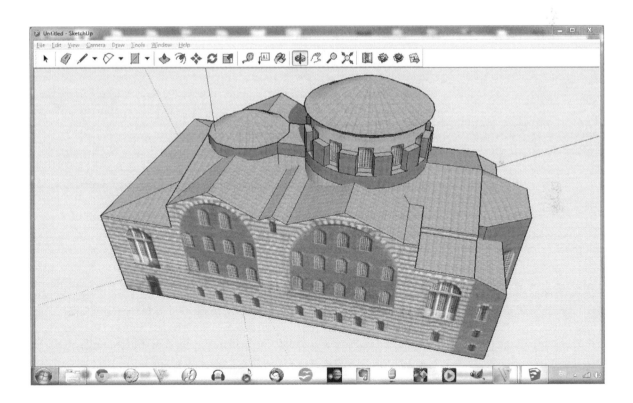

Tinkercad

Cloud-based – runs in some browsers

www.tinkercad.com

Tinkercad is perhaps the easiest CAD program available and a good place to start making simple 3D designs. However, you may run into the limits of the software all too quickly, and it's not clear that the application will continue to have a free version. It was recently purchased by AutoDesk and the website says "Free (for a limited time only!)." Tinkercad has the ability to import 2D and 3D files, and a set of fun tutorials to take you through the basics of 3D design. There are also premium features for groups of accounts. The website terms of service prohibit users under the age of 13.

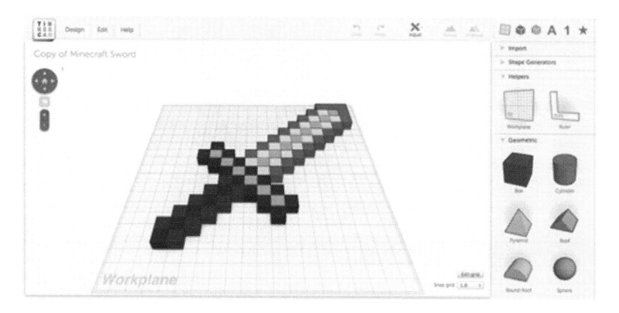

A note on cloud-based CAD programs

Be aware that there are pros and cons to cloud-based software. Having the program in the cloud eliminates the need to install software, since the program runs in the browser, and perhaps even on tablets and netbooks. Your students can have their own accounts and access them from anywhere, if you accept the terms of use. Your school will need to have good bandwidth, and your browsers must work with WebGL.

At this time, only Chrome and Firefox browsers have WebGL (not Microsoft browsers). Even with supported browsers, you may see lags in dragging objects and points across the screen, which is frustrating when trying to design. There may be outages with these services, which make them unavailable at inconvenient times. These services may also change the terms, interface, or features without notice, including just disappearing.

3DTin

Cloud-based – runs in some browsers

www.3dtin.com

3DTin is nearly as easy to use as TinkerCAD, but has more features. It lets you create projects from scratch using a library of geometric shapes. Our experience is that it is easier to align parts in 3DTin than it is in TinkerCAD. 3DTin lets you download your drawing as an STL file ready to print. 3DTin is free, however, there is a premium fee for importing files, additional file management, having an ad free interface, and a few other features. Be sure to check the website as the program was recently sold to a new company, and there may be other changes.

Autodesk 123D

Mac, Windows, iPad, and Cloud, depending on application

www.123dapp.com

Autodesk is one of the premiere publishers of computer-aided design software. Their products are found in design firms and architects' offices all over the world.

Autodesk supports the beginning 3D designer with a rich suite of tools that covers the gamut from parts designed from geometric pieces, to the more organic designs suitable for modeling living organisms. In fact, Clark Barnett, a teacher in the Conejo Valley Unified School District in California does a project with his kids using one of the Autodesk applications on the iPad – 123D Creature. With this tool, students design their own insects that could live in the ecosystem of their classroom. Once printed, these "insects" are mounted in a display tray and students explain why their insect is likely to survive on its own in the classroom ecosystem.

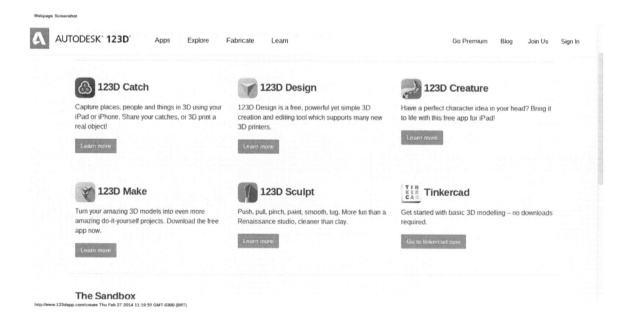

Meshmixer

Mac, Windows

www.meshmixer.com

Meshmixer lets you sculpt by hand as if you were working with clay, making it perfect for creating organic, rather than geometric, shapes. Anyone who has worked with modeling clay will know how to use the tools in this program, and there is a great manual to show exactly how to get the most from it. Tools like this can be used to bring 3D printing into the life sciences classroom.

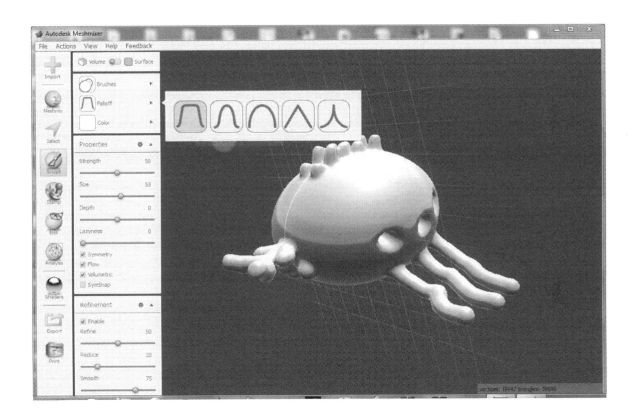

Sculptris

Mac, Windows

www.pixologic.com/sculptris

This amazing tool is a great next step for *Meshmixer* users. It was designed for sculptors (and would-be sculptors). Instead of a blank screen, you are presented with a round ball of "clay" that can be shaped into just about anything you want. While not geared toward the creation of geometric objects, it is a perfect tool for building models of various creatures – both real and imagined. Finished projects are exported as OBJ files that can be easily converted to STL files by Meshlab (see below). Once you start working with this tool, hours happily go by as you create amazing things, all of which can be built on your 3D printer. This software comes with good documentation and links to some video tutorials we highly recommend for anyone interested in this tool.

KnotPlot

Mac, Windows

www.knotplot.com

This program lets you build mathematical knots of all kinds. While created for math geeks, knots are pretty to look at, and students can use this program to explore this branch of mathematics – a worthwhile activity in itself. One great feature of this program is that it lets you export your image as an STL file directly and send it to your printer software with no further work required. Finished knots can be sent out for metal plating in case you want to make your own jewelry. (One provider of this service can be found at www.repliforminc.com/RePliKote.htm.)

MeshLab

Mac, Windows, Linux

meshlab.sourceforge.net

Sometimes (as with Sculptris), your 3D images will be exported as OBJ files that need to be converted to STL files so they can be printed. MeshLab does this job beautifully and even lets you adjust the mesh from which the model is defined to optimize it for printing. This optimization process lets you clean up your model so it will print perfectly. Another useful function of this program is that it lets you import several STL files you can assemble into one piece that can be exported and printed. This is particularly useful when you want to adapt an existing part to connect it with another one you've saved as a separate file. We will use this tool for this purpose in some of our projects.

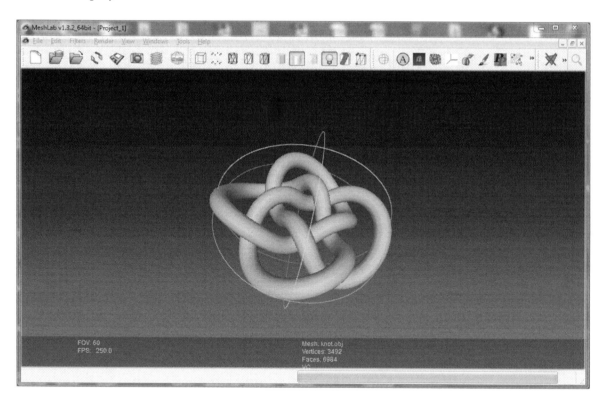

And there are more good programs coming out all the time, so keep your eyes open and let us know what you find (3D@knights-of-knowledge.com)!

Capturing 3D Images From Objects

Affordable and reliable 3D scanners are just becoming available for hobbyists and schools. For example, the Makerbot digitizer (store.makerbot.com/digitizer) currently retails for about $800, and makes very good scans of small objects.

This scanner uses two laser beams and a rotating plate to scan the object from all angles and then generates an STL file for use with your printer. The process takes about 12 minutes, and the quality is accurate within about 2 mm. The only concern with this (and other) laser scanners is that it needs to be placed in a location where the laser beams don't hit your eyes directly. Information on all of this is explored in the operation manual.

Without a scanner, it is still possible to "scan" a physical object in order to print it. One approach is to take multiple photographs of the object at different angles with your digital camera, and then using software tools like 123D Catch (www.123dapp.com/catch) or VisualSFM (ccwu.me/vsfm), build a 3D model that can be exported as an STL file for printing. It turns out that this approach, while possible, is trickier than it sounds.

An easier approach is to use the Microsoft Kinect connected to your computer and use the Scenect software (www.faro.com/scenect/scenect) to scan and build your model. While this process works, the models don't have very good resolution and the setup is a bit cumbersome.

Of course the real question is, why are 3D digitizers a good idea in the first place?

When youngsters make sculptures out of clay, the objects tend to fall apart after awhile. If you scan a clay model though, when it is printed in plastic, students can paint it and place it in a class project, or take it home! The creativity comes in the sculpting. All the digitizer does is allow the model to be made out of plastic.

Projects

Project	Software
1 – Gear Board	Inkscape, OpenSCAD
2 – Backpack Tag	Inkscape, OpenSCAD, Meshlab
3 – Backpack Tag Using Tinkercad	Tinkercad
4 – Tangrams	Inkscape
5 – Fan-Powered Car	Inkscape, OpenSCAD, Meshlab
6 – Tensegrity Models for Polyhedra	Inkscape, OpenSCAD
7 – Two-Gear Clock	Inkscape, OpenSCAD
8 – Pentagonal Tiles	Inkscape, OpenSCAD
9 – Pentagrams	Inkscape, OpenSCAD
10 – Exploring Knots	KnotPlot
11 – Designing Creatures	Meshmixer
12 – Printing Your Own Fossils	Meshlab
13 – Designing a Mobile Sculpture	Inkscape, OpenSCAD, Meshlab
14 – Making Escher-Style Tiles	SketchUp Make
15 – Making a Box for Electronic Projects	Inkscape, OpenSCAD, Meshlab
16 – Towers of Hanoi	Inkscape, OpenSCAD, Meshlab
17 – Making a Greek Temple	SketchUp Make
18 – Designing Your Own Pottery	Let's Create! Pottery

1 – Gear Board

Design and build a board with plastic gears to explore the mathematics of gear design.

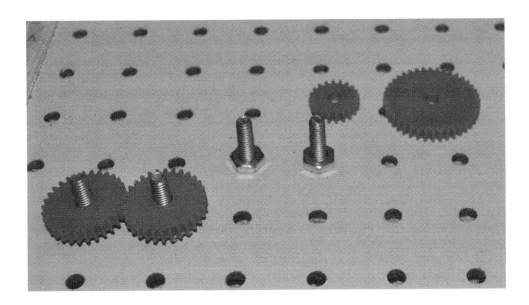

Background

Gear boards are popular tools to help young children learn the basics of rotary motion. Assorted gears can be designed to represent different gear ratios, and then scaled to fit the pegboard centers (every inch) with a hole in the center for #12 screw (.25"). All the materials can be found at a hardware store.

Gears are very useful things to make for use in robotics projects. Inkscape makes it very easy for you to create accurate gears for your work.

NGSS Areas

Disciplinary Core Idea(s):

- Physical Science
- Engineering

How Scientists and Engineers Work

- Tinkering and experimentation

CCSS Math Connections

- Make sense of problems and persevere in solving them.
- Reason abstractly and quantitatively.
- Model with mathematics.
- Use appropriate tools strategically.
- Attend to precision.
- Look for and make use of structure.
- Look for and express regularity in repeated reasoning.

Materials

- 3/16" peg board sheet cut into 1 foot squares
- 10 #12 x 1" screws
- 10 #12 hex nuts

Construction details

1. Download and install the Inkscape software.
2. Download and install the OpenSCAD software.
3. Download and place the contents of the Paths2openscad folder inside the Inkscape\share\ extensions folder inside the Programs folder on your computer.
4. Download and install the Meshlab software.
5. Open Inkscape.
6. Under the Extensions menu, choose Render and then Gear. That brings up a screen for your gear's data.
7. Choose the number of teeth (24 is fine for now).
8. Click Apply and close the Gear window.

9.   Select the gear drawing by clicking on a gear tooth with the mouse. Click on the Zoom to fit the drawing in the window on the right tool bar to see a larger image.

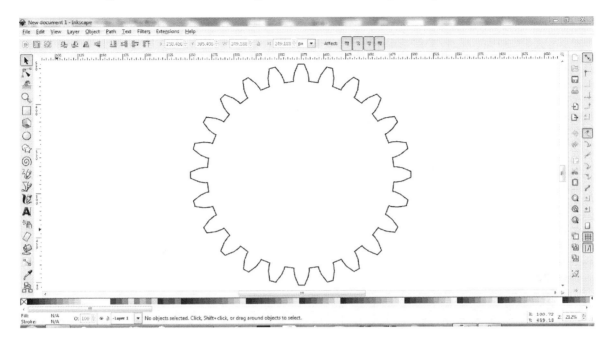

10. Choose a fill color you like from the color palette at the bottom (color doesn't matter at this point).

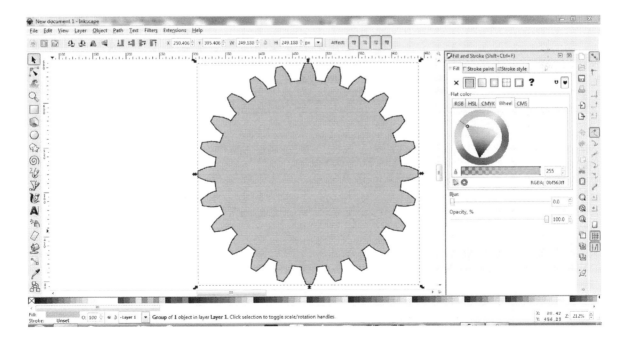

11. You want your gears to fit together on a pegboard with one-inch centers. This means the gear diameter has to be a little bigger than one inch so the teeth will mesh properly with other gears. Don't make the gear too large, or it will not fit! A diameter of about 1.075" works pretty well. With the gear selected, go to the second layer of the menu bar where you see some numbers representing the width and height of the selected object. If the measurement units are pixels (px), change this to inches (in), click the lock icon, and type in the desired size of your gear in the W box (1.075 ").

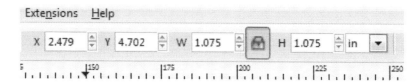

12. Go to the Object menu and select Ungroup (this is needed for the next step to work).

13. Now your gear needs a hole in the middle to connect to a motor shaft or some other part of your project. Outside the drawing area, choose the circle tool and draw a small oval (we will turn it into a circle of the correct size next).

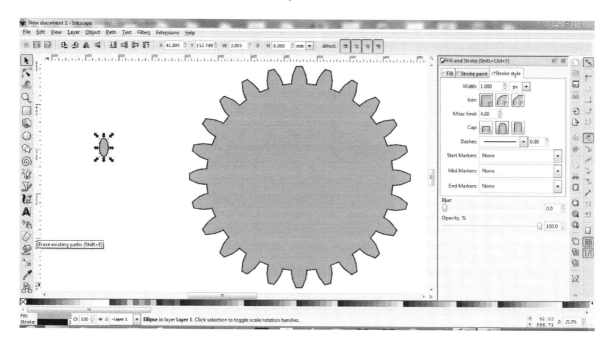

14. Click on the Selection tool (arrow at the top of the left column). With the oval selected, go to the second layer of the menu bar and unlock the lock by clicking on the lock icon, and type in the desired size of your gear's hole in the W and H boxes. For a #12 screw, this would be 0.25 inches for both the width and the height.

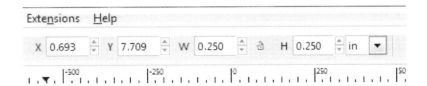

15. Next, drag the hole over your gear image and place it near the center. It doesn't have to be perfect – we will position it accurately next.

16. Select the circle image and then click on the gear so that both circle and gear are selected. Go to the Object menu and choose Align and Distribute. From this box (on the right), click on Center on vertical axis (top row; third from the left), and then click on Center on horizontal axis (second row; third from the left). Your circle will now be exactly centered on the gear.

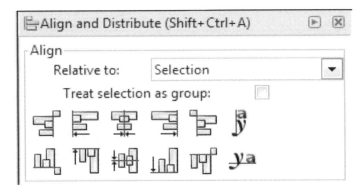

17. Now we need to create a hole where the inner circle is. To do this, be sure both the gear and the circle are selected, and from the Path menu, choose Difference (Ctrl +). If everything went according to plan, you now have a hole in the center of your gear! SAVE YOUR WORK! For example, save the art as [mygears.svg].

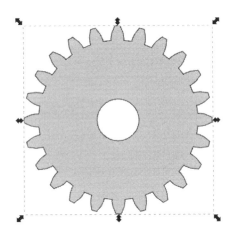

18. Now that you have a two-dimensional picture of your gear, you can make several copies (start with four) with the Copy and Paste commands so multiple gears print at the same time. Leave a little space between the gears to make them easy to separate after they are printed.

19. It is time to extrude the gears into a shape your 3D printer can make. To do this, select all the gears (Ctrl-A) and from the Extensions menu, choose Generate from Path, and Paths to OpenSCAD. If everything works, you will see a window open that will let you add thickness to your gear. Choose the thickness you want – 5mm, for example, and then choose an output file name such as [~/desktop/gear.scad] and click Apply, and then Done. This will generate a file you can open in OpenSCAD. You are close to having your project finished!

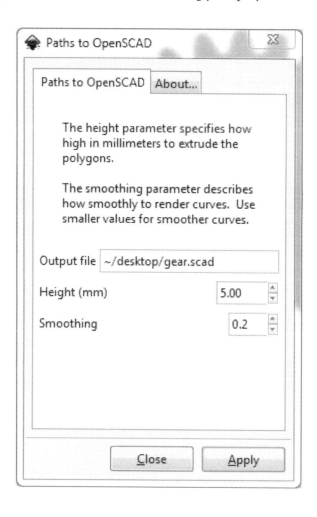

20. Close Inkscape and then open the OpenSCAD file you just created. This shows a lot of text, but no image. To fix that, go to the Design menu and choose Compile and Render (F6). Your finished gear will now show up as a 3D object you can rotate with your mouse to examine from different angles.

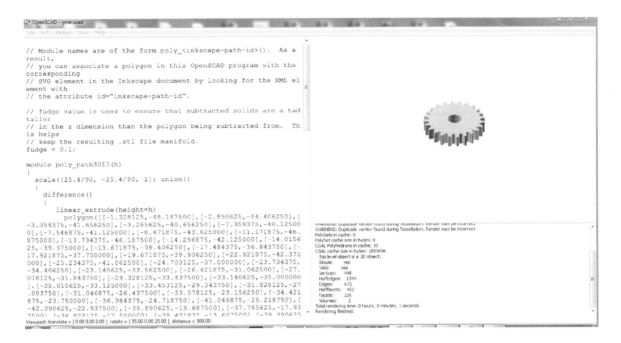

21. As your final step, go to the Design menu and choose Export as STL, and save the file on your desktop where it is easy to find, [gears.stl], for example. STL stands for "stereolithography," and is the format your 3D printer will use to generate the file it needs to build your finished part!

This project involved a lot of steps, but once you get going with these tools, everything will come naturally and you'll be designing other amazing parts in no time!

Things to do and notice

- We are surrounded by gears in everything from clocks to automobiles. The best way to understand how gears work is to build your own sets and see how they move when meshed together. Some of the following activities require that you modify the designs and print new gears.

- Assemble a pattern of interlocking gears of the same size. What do you notice about the directions of rotation when you turn one gear?

- Assemble a pattern of interlocking gears with different sizes. Count the number of teeth in each gear in a pair, and then notice how many times the smaller gear rotates when the large gear is rotated once. How is this related to the number of teeth in each gear? (Put a dot of color on one tooth on each gear to make it easy to count the rotations.)

- Build gears that would work on the diagonals of your board.

- What if the hole in the gear is off center? Can two gears with the same off-center hole locations still mesh properly?

- Create a gear arrangement in which the gears are arranged in a triangular pattern. Can the gears turn? Why or why not?

2 – Backpack Tag

Make an identification tag with your name on it in embossed letters for your backpack.

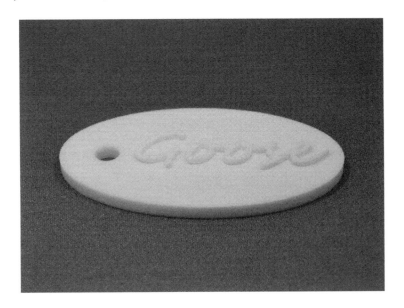

Background

3D printers are perfect for making small personalized items. This project is one that lets kids create things they can use every day.

NGSS Areas

Disciplinary Core Idea(s)

- Engineering

How Scientists and Engineers Work

- Tinkering and experimentation

CCSS Math Connections

None

Construction details

1. Open Inkscape.

2. Use the circle tool to draw an oval with a nice shape for your backpack tag. Be sure the oval is filled with any color you choose, selected from the color bar at the bottom of the screen. This forms the base of the tag. (**The actual color will depend on the color plastic you use in your 3D printer.**)

3. On the right tool bar, click on the tool that says "Zoom to fit drawing in window."

4. To adjust the size of your oval, select the Arrow (Selection tool at top of the left tool bar), and click on the oval. Change the size of the oval by dragging any corner of the selected oval.

5. Right below the menu options at the top of the screen, you will see rectangles with numbers indicating X,Y,W,H, and units. Go to the units window and choose millimeters (the default is px for pixels). Note that all the other numbers change.

6. Adjust width and height: set the width for 90 mm or less. Set the height for no higher than 90 as well. When you adjust the width, the height will change. You can manually change either number – and you will notice that your oval changes shape to correspond to the numbers. You can also manipulate the oval, and the numbers will change.

7. Click outside the oval and draw a circle that will become the hole for a strap to hold the tag to your backpack, using the circle tool.

8. Click on the Selection tool; click on the oval, and adjust the height and width (5 mm is a good number) for the size of the hole you want.

9. Change the color of your circle so that you will be able to see it when it is on top of your oval.

10. Drag the circle on top of the oval, in a position that looks nice!

11. To adjust, select the circle; hold the shift key down and select the oval by clicking on it.

12. On the menu bar, choose Object, then Align and Distribute, or press Shift-Ctrl-A, which opens the Align and Distribute Panel on the right side of the screen.

13. Click on the Center on Horizontal Axis image (second row, third image from the left), and voilà! Your circle will be aligned.

14. With both objects selected, go to the Path menu, and choose Difference (Ctrl -). This creates a hole in your tag.

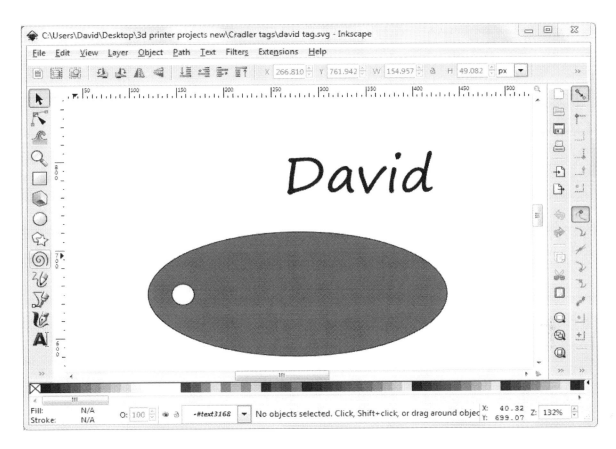

15. If you need to zoom out, giving you more space, press the minus (-) key; to zoom in, press Shift and the plus (+) key.

16. Click outside the oval; click on the text tool on the left (the big A), and start typing your name. To change the font and size, select your name, and choose the font and size you want from the top menu bar. You will find that things work best if you bold your text. (Experiment with different typefaces to find those that work best for you.)

17. To get a sense of how your name will look on the luggage tag, select it with the Selection tool and place it on the oval. Continue adjusting size until you're happy with how it looks. To maintain the aspect ratio, click on the little lock between the width and height boxes at the top of the screen. (The tag will look best from a design angle if you type no more than your first and last names, no more than two lines on the tag – first names by themselves look even better!)

18. When you're done, drag your name off the oval.

19. Inkscape drawings that are going to be extruded have to be graphic objects. To turn your text into a graphic object, select it and go to the Path menu, choose Object to Path (first option in this menu – Shift-Ctrl-C). The result will be a collection of graphic objects representing your name.

20. SAVE YOUR WORK! Save as [yournametag.svg] on the desktop.

21. Now you are ready to export to OpenSCAD. You will be exporting two objects separately: the tag, and your name. Be sure to use different names for the two extrusions as you export them!

22. Select the tag and go to the Extensions menu; click on Generate from Path, and Paths to OpenSCAD. A window will pop up, giving you the option to name your file. Name your file: [~/desktop/tag base.scad]. Adjust the height to 5mm (leave Smoothing at 0.2). Click on Apply. Close the window.

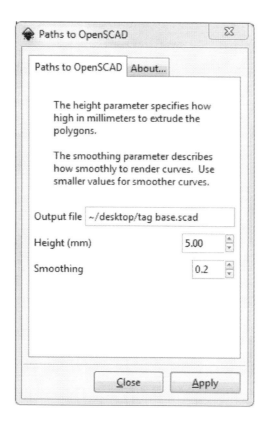

23. Repeat for your name. Select your name, go the Extensions menu; click on Generate from Path, and Paths to OpenSCAD. A window will pop up, giving you the option to name your file. Name your file: [~/desktop/yourname.scad]. Adjust the height to 3 mm (leave Smoothing at 0.2). Click on Apply. Close the window.

24. Quit Inkscape; you will see the .svg and the two .scad files on your desktop.

25. Double click on one of the .scad files. Click on Design from the top menu; and choose Compile and Render (F6). Now you will be able to see your object. Feel free to rotate it with your mouse and see what it looks like from different orientations. During the rendering process, you may see "error" messages in the box below your object. Ignore them!

26. Go back to the Design menu, and Export as STL. Choose where you want to save it, and click Save.

27. Repeat this process with the second .scad file.

28. Close OpenSCAD.

29. On the desktop you will see the files you just exported.

30. Launch Meshnet.

31. Import both STL files into Meshnet by clicking on the Import Mesh folder icon in the toolbar. When you import both files, you will not see the one with your name because it is exactly the same height as the tag base file. By the way, when Meshnet imports files, it also cleans them up of unneeded parts sometimes left behind by OpenSCAD. This is a great feature since it makes your final prints look better.

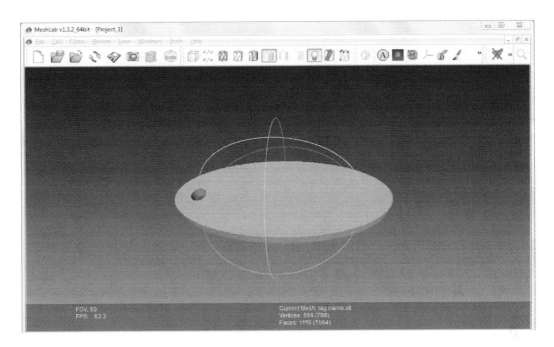

32. Next you will want to raise the text a bit from the top of the tag. To do this, click on the toolbar icon near the right side that looks like three coordinates. This brings up a dialog to allow (among other things) translations. Press the T key and drag the mouse upward on the vertical arrow until the text is at the right height. You can also move the text left to right to center it on the tag if you wish. Before closing this dialog box by clicking on the coordinates icon button again, be sure you have saved your changes for the translation.

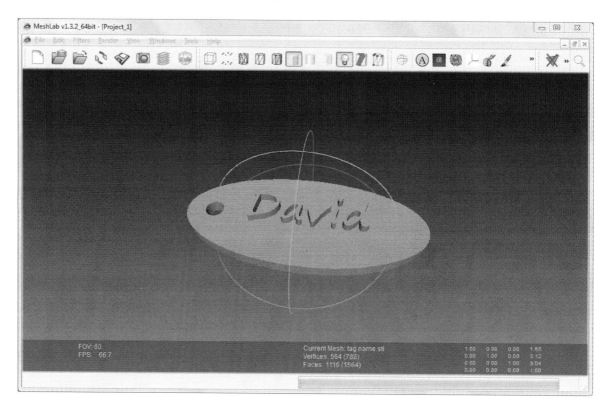

33. While your tag looks finished on the screen, the image still has two separate parts (the base and the name). You need to merge these into one part before exporting the file to print it. To do this, notice the toolbar icon to the right of the camera image – it looks like a stack of papers. Click on this bar and you will see a new window appear on the right of the screen showing information about each layer.

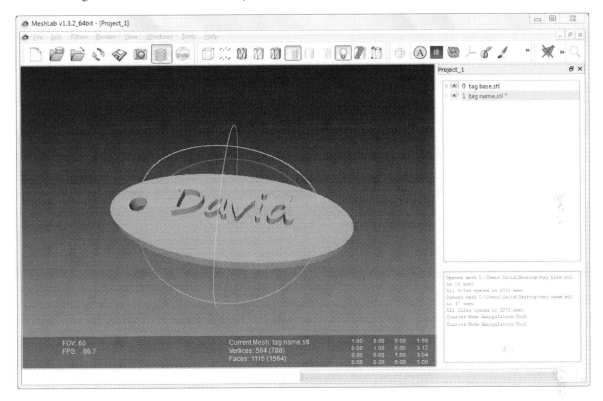

34. Right-click your mouse on one of the layer names and this will bring up some options, one of which is to flatten the image. Choose this option and your image will be bound together as one object. Note that, in the process of doing this, Meshlab will also clean up the final image to remove any duplicate parts.

35. Export this merged file to an STL file by clicking on the disk icon in the toolbar and print your tag.

Things to do and notice

- This activity is designed to develop some basic skills with the software used in many projects. The following questions involve the design and fabrication of different tags.

- Do all typefaces work well when printed in 3D?

- How do you select the best typeface to use?

- Suppose you want your name in a different color than that of the tag. How would you do that?

3 – Making a Backpack Tag with Tinkercad

Design and build a backpack tag using Tinkercad.

Background

Previously we made a backpack tag using Inkscape, OpenSCAD, and Meshlab as our tools. This project creates a similar tag with a cloud-based program, Tinkercad.

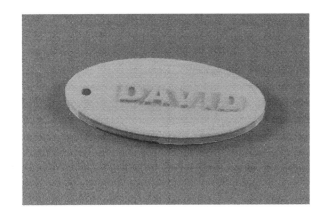

NGSS Areas

How Scientists and Engineers Work:
- Tinkering and experimentation

CCSS Math Connections

- None

Construction details

1. Launch Tinkercad at www.tinkercad.com

2. Log in to your account, or create a new account if you are a new user.

3. Create a new design. Note that Tinkercad will automatically give your design a unique name of its own choosing.

4. To make the base of the tag, click on the cylinder shape and drag it to the center of the workspace.

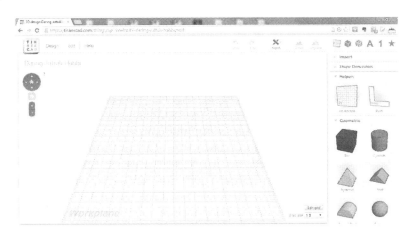

5. Grab one of the square boxes at the bottom of the cylinder and drag it to create an oval 90 mm wide and 50 mm deep.

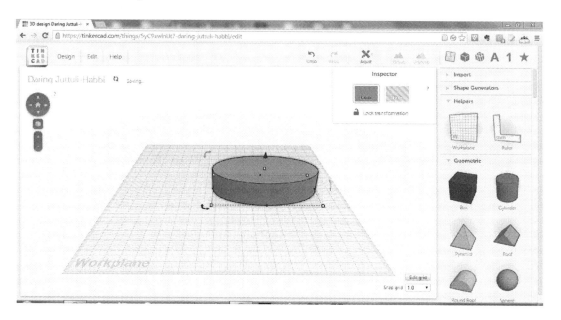

6. To change the thickness of the tag, click on the center white square box at the top of the cylinder, and drag it down to a height of 5 mm.

7. To create a name, click on the A button at the top right of the window. This brings up a block letter alphabet (Tinkercad does not support multiple typefaces at this time.).

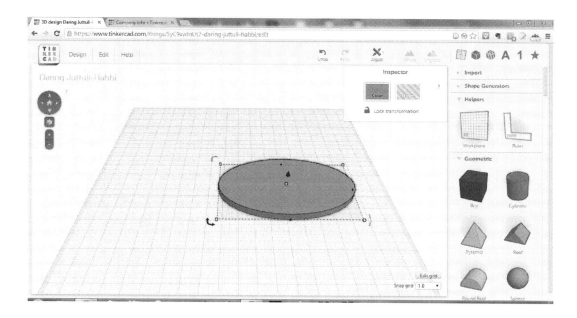

8. Drag the letters of your name onto a blank area of the workplace one at a time. Don't worry about the spacing or alignment at this time.

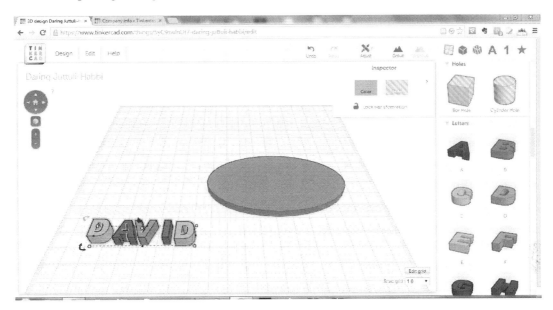

9. Select all the letters, and using the center white square at the top of the letters, pull the thickness from 4 mm to 7 mm so they will be extending a little from the top of the tag.

10. With all the letters selected, click on the Adjust button at the top of the screen and choose Align. This brings up a series of vertical and horizontal dots. As you move your mouse over the dot to the bottom left of the text, it will change color. Click on this dot to align the text vertically.

11. With the text selected, drag it to the position you want on the tag and unselect the text.

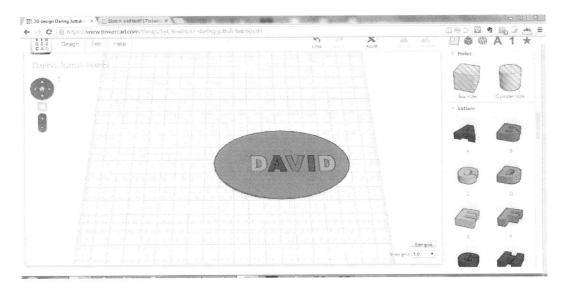

12. Choosing one letter at a time, select it and, using the left and right arrow keys, move it to the correct position to balance the letters properly.

13. Next, to make the hole in the tag, drag another cylinder to the workplace and adjust its diameter to 5 mm. Don't worry about the height since this will be turned into a hole.

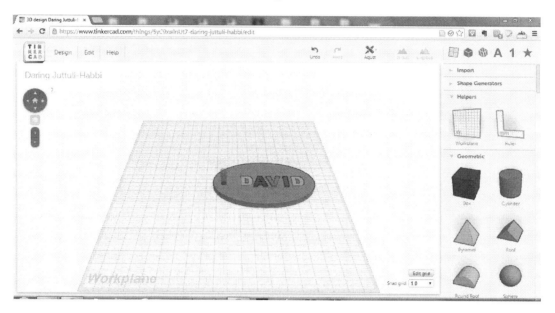

14. Click on the Hole style in the inspector box at the top right of the workplace.

15. You are done! Click on the design menu and choose Download for 3D Printing and save your STL file. After it is saved, you will want to rename it to something you will remember – [Tinkercadtag.stl], for example.

You can see what your tag looks like by opening it in Meshlab. Notice that all the colors of your original picture are gone. They are just in the original to make it easy for you to see everything.

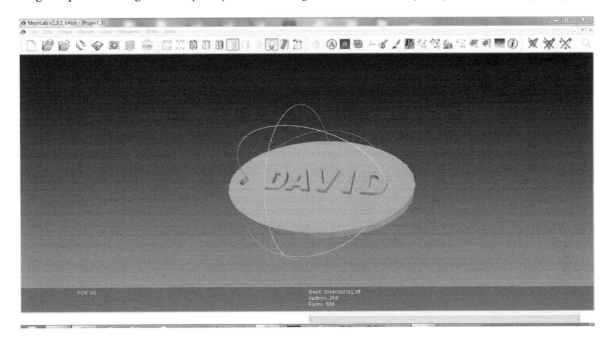

Things to Do and Notice

- Compare this method of making a backpack tag to the one made using Inkscape and OpenSCAD. Which method is easier for you?

- What advantages does each approach have?

4 – Tangrams

Design and build a Tangram set.

Background

Tangrams have been popular puzzles for hundreds of years, and inexpensive tangram sets are easy to find. Tangram sets consist of seven pieces – five isosceles triangles, one square, and one parallelogram. The completed puzzle uses all seven pieces without overlapping to complete a design.

The advantage in designing your own set is that it lets you learn the geometric relationship between the tiles in ways that may not be apparent if you only work with pre-designed tiles. In designing the parts in Inkscape, it is easiest to design the pieces so they fit into a square that can be printed out all at once.

NGSS Areas

Disciplinary Core Idea(s):

- Engineering

How Scientists and Engineers Work:

- Look for patterns

CCSS Math Connections

- Make sense of problems and persevere in solving them.

- Reason abstractly and quantitatively.

- Model with mathematics.

- Use appropriate tools strategically.

- Attend to precision.

- Look for and make use of structure.

Construction details

1. Open Inkscape. With the Rectangle and square tool (F4), draw a 10 cm square (select millimeters from the bar below the menus at the top). Then using the image below, observe what you can about the triangles first.

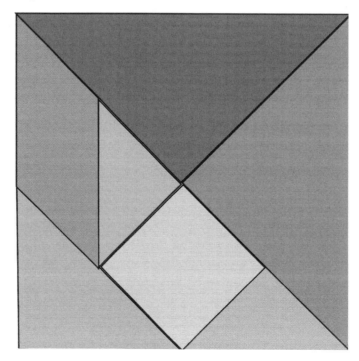

2. Start by drawing the triangle at the lower left corner in your square. The vertical and horizontal sides of the triangle are the same: 5 cm. To draw the triangle, select Inkscape's "Draw Bezier curves and straight lines" tool (Shift-F6) on the left menu. Create a triangle of any size, using the edges of the square as guides. To use this tool, click once (anywhere on the screen) to set the first point in your triangle. Move some distance, click again (don't worry about the length or if the line is perfectly vertical). Then go down to the right to draw the third point; click. Finally, go back to the starting point – which will change color when you are over it – and click again. This will create your first triangle (which is probably the wrong size and has inexact angles at this point).

3. Move this triangle onto the square so that the bottom left corner of the triangle exactly touches the bottom left corner of the square.

4. Using the Edit paths by nodes tool underneath the Selection tool on the left column (F2), click on the top dot of the triangle and drag so that it perfectly aligns with the vertical edge of the square. Repeat for the corner on the lower right of the triangle.

5. Click the Selection tool; choose 50 mm in the boxes for width and height at the top, under the menu bar. You may see that the corners at the upper left and the lower right of the triangle are not perfectly aligned, so repeat the adjustments you performed earlier.

6. When you are finished with your adjustments, double check that both width and height are 50 mm.

7. Except for size and rotation, all the other triangles have the same proportions as this one. The tricky part is rotating this triangle 45 degrees so the base is parallel to one of the sides of the square.

8. First, make a copy of your triangle, select it, paste a copy and then click on the copy to select it.. This changes the corner arrows to turn arrows.

9. Dragging on one of these turn arrows rotates the image by an arbitrary amount. (Do not do this!) If you do rotate the triangle a bit, from the Edit menu choose Undo rotate. We want an exact 45 degree rotation. The secret tip here is to hold the control key down while rotating the image. This restricts the turning angles to increments of 15 degrees, giving us 45 degrees very easily!

10. Once you have done this, use the Rotate selection tool by 90 degrees clockwise on the line under the menu bar until the copied triangle looks like a triangular hat.

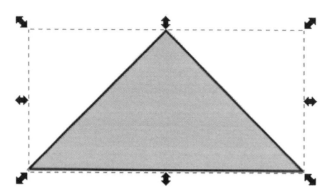

11. Select this triangle and click on the lock between the W and H fields on the line below the menu bar.

12. Set the width to 100 mm.

13. Make a copy of this triangle and paste it on the screen.

14. Using the Rotate selection tool by 90 degrees clockwise, turn both the large triangles so they fit in place on the top and right side of the original square.

15. The remaining shapes (square, parallelogram and two small triangles) are all made from small triangles, so we will make a small triangle shape first.

16. Start with the triangle at the bottom right. This is just like the top triangle, but with a base of 50mm. Copy the large triangle, paste a copy, and then resize it to 50mm and place it on the bottom right of the square.

17. Next, make several copies of this triangle and place them on the screen.

18. To make the square, put two of the small triangles together. Use the arrow keys to make fine adjustments in the position so the triangles just overlap.

19. Next, with both triangles still selected, go to the Path menu and choose Union. This locks the two triangles into one piece. If you see a line between the two triangles, undo this step and adjust the overlap to the point where this line does not show up when Union is selected.

20. Place the remaining triangle next to the square, and build the parallelogram in the same manner we built the square. Once you are done, you need to join the triangles in the parallelogram with the Path menu Union tool.

21. Before putting the parallelogram in place, remove the square you made at the start of this project.

22. Finally, move the pieces apart from each other enough to make them easy to separate after printing. This is not an exact amount. The following picture can be a guide.

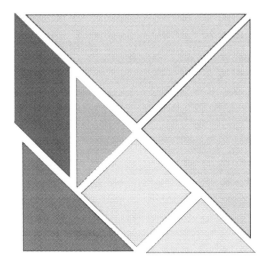

23. Select all the pieces and, using the Paths to OpenSCAD tool, extrude them by (for example) 3 or 4 mm. This gives a nice thickness to each piece when they are printed.

24. The final drawing for the 3D model (using an extrusion length of 3mm) looks like this:

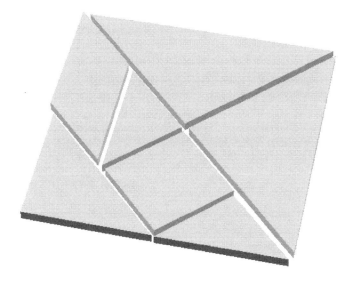

25. Next, export to an STL file and print the Tangram set on your 3D printer!

Things to do and notice

- Find Tangram challenges online and build the shapes using your set of pieces. (For example, tangrams.ca/tangram-assorted has a good collection. Remember that all seven pieces must be used in each picture.

- How can the set be modified by adding other pieces?

- Build a new set with your own pieces and experiment to build various objects.

- Print sets with different colors, then mix the sets so all the triangles have the same color, and the other shapes have a different one. This may make final projects more engaging to younger learners while reinforcing shape names.

5 – Fan Powered Car

Design and build a fan-powered car. This project uses parts made with the 3D printer, an electric motor, and a battery pack to power the motor, and a few nails to act as the car axles.

Background

3D printers can be used to make cars, boats, and other moving objects. The performance of the finished project depends on many variables, each of which can be tested.

NGSS Areas

Disciplinary Core Idea(s):

- Physical Science
- Engineering

How Scientists and Engineers Work:

- Tinkering and experimentation
- Modeling

CCSS Math Connections

- Make sense of problems and persevere in solving them.
- Reason abstractly and quantitatively.
- Construct viable arguments and critique the reasoning of others.
- Model with mathematics.
- Use appropriate tools strategically.
- Attend to precision.
- Look for and make use of structure.

Materials

Except for the batteries, the electronic parts are very inexpensive and can be found online at electronics suppliers such as www.AllElectronics.com.

- Battery holder for 2 AA cells
- Two AA batteries
- One small DC motor that works well on 3 volts
- 2D x one-inch roofing nails (these are used as axles and have a large enough head to keep the wheels from coming off.
- Glue gun, soldering iron, solder, 28 gauge insulated wire. (The wire and soldering iron are optional.)

> **Note** – This project may involve some soldering, so that task should be done under adult supervision. Soldering the connections makes them more reliable, but the project can be completed using other methods to secure the battery leads.

Construction details

Like some of our other projects, this one uses Inkscape, OpenSCAD and Meshlab. There are three steps to this project:

- Designing and building the car chassis
- Designing and building the propeller
- Assembling the car

Designing and building the car chassis

1. Open Inkscape.

2. The car chassis needs to be big enough to hold the batteries and the motor. You might start with a rectangular shape 5 cm wide and 9 cm long. In designing this shape, you might also want to put some marks at the points where you want to put the wheels.

3. On the same drawing, create four wheels. The wheels can be any size you want. We used 2 cm as the diameter, but feel free to experiment with another size if you wish. The hole in the center of the wheel should be just large enough for the wheel to spin smoothly on the axle we will make with the nails, but not so large as to let the wheel wobble. You may need to experiment a bit to get this just right.

4. Save your file as [fan car.svg].

5. As for the motor, this needs to be put on a pillar that extends from the chassis. We chose to use an oval-shaped pillar 20 mm wide and 18 mm high to hold the motor to minimize the blocking of air for the fan blade. Select the oval and extrude it to a height of 25 mm with the Paths to OpenSCAD command found in the Extensions menu inside the Generate from Path setting. Save the OpenSCAD file on the desktop as [pillar.scad].

6. Next, group the chassis and four wheels together compactly, and extrude them to Open SCAD by 3 mm. Export this to the desktop as [chassis.scad]. When you are done, you will have two OpenSCAD files – one for the chassis and wheels, and one for the motor pillar.

7. Our next step it to assemble the two parts into a complete design, and for this we will use Meshlab.

8. Launch Meshlab and choose Import from the File menu. Select the STL file with the model for the chassis and wheels.

9. Import the pillar STL file. You will see the pillar rising out from the chassis. Next, select the translate tool (the one with four arrows) and drag the pillar up a bit until the bottom of the pillar is embedded in the chassis by about 1 mm. This insures that the pillar is firmly embedded in the chassis when it is printed.

10. Next, go to the top view of the drawing and move the pillar to the end of the chassis, and center it on the top and bottom of the chassis image. The final image might look like the image on the next page in isometric view.

11. Finally, export your finished car body and wheels as an STL file.

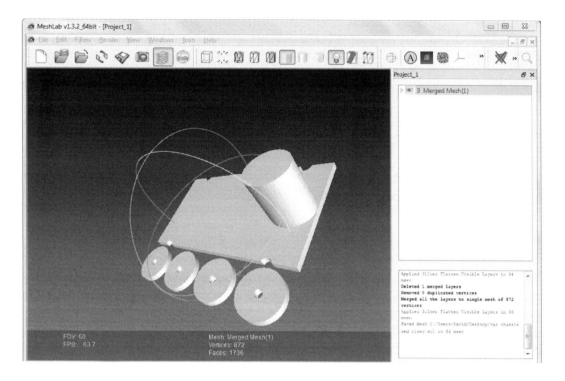

Designing and building the propeller

12. A propeller can be tricky to design, so we will use one found at www.thingiverse.com/
    thing:116410. (This website is an amazing repository of 3D objects you can download and
    print. You can even add your own designs to the collection if you wish.) When you download
    all the files, there is one that we will use right away: the file named [propellerbetter2.scad]. You
    will be editing this file to make the exact propeller you want. When you open the SCAD file
    you will see some variables listed on the left panel. Open SCAD models like this one that are
    easy to edit are called "parametric designs" because they contain parameters (variables) you
    can change to customize the model to your needs.

```
//Parametric propeller using flat plates (with cylindrical end)
for fins
//There are probably better ways to do this.
//Creative Commons license.

fs=1;  //default $fs is 2, is the min facet size
fa=4;  //default $fa is 12, is # of degrees per facet
trad=23.5; //outerradius not counting outw. 23.5 good
outw=1.5; //outerwidth. 1.5 is good
nfins=3; //number of fins. Min # is 2, but 3 is better
rins= 5; //radius of coupling thing, 5 is good
tdepth = 3; //depth of prop. reduce if nfins is big, 3 good
fangle = 40; //angle of fins, 40 is good for printing
tfin = 1; //thickness of fins, 1 is good
```

13. The main variables you will want to play with are: "trad" (the outer radius of the propeller), which we set to 40; "nfins" sets the number of fins on the propeller, which we set to 6; "rins" is the radius of the hub at the center of the propeller, and we set this to 7. (You should experiment with different propellers.) When you compile and display the file with the variables we just set, you get the following image.

14. Now the only problem with this propeller is that there is no hole in the base of the hub to fit over the motor shaft. You could drill a hole, but it is easy to design a bushing with the right sized hole in the center. A bushing is a small ring that will fit in between the propeller hub and the motor, so the shaft fits through it. Save this propeller image as an STL file with a name like [propeller.stl].

15. Using Inkscape, design a bushing with a diameter of 1 cm and a hole just a bit smaller than the diameter of the motor shaft. If your motor shaft is 2 mm in diameter, make the hole 1.8 or 1.9 mm in diameter so the shaft fits tightly when you press it in place. Export this image to OpenSCAD using a thickness of, for example, 3 mm. From OpenSCAD, compile and display the image and export it as an STL file with a name like [bushing.stl].

16. Now you can "mesh" the propeller and the bushing so that they are one piece.

17. Using Meshlab, import both STL files, and lift the propeller enough to reveal the bushing underneath, but not so far that the bushing separates from the propeller.

18. Flatten the image and export the combined mesh with a name like [final propeller.stl] and print the propeller.

19. After printing, you need to peel away the base layer (called a raft) that appears in all your designs. When doing this, be careful as you get close to the bushing, as it may pop off. If it does, just glue it back in place with a glue gun.

Assembling the car

20. To assemble the car, use a glue gun to glue the propeller to the motor shaft. Put the wheels on each of the four nails and glue the nails so they are centered on the cutouts on the chassis. Be sure the wheels are free to turn, but not so far away from the base that they can wobble a lot. Next, glue the battery holder to the base to the right of the riser, and glue the motor to the top of the riser with the propeller facing the back of the car.

21. Connect the battery to the motor and see if the propeller is blowing air to the back. If not, reverse the battery leads. Solder one of the battery leads to the motor connector. If you have a small slide switch, you can connect one side to the other motor connector and the other side to the remaining wire in the battery pack. Otherwise, you can start the motor just by wrapping the remaining battery pack wire to the open connector on the motor.

22. If everything works, you car will move forward when the motor spins. If it doesn't move very well, make sure the wheels turn smoothly, and experiment with the size and number of blades on the propeller. This kind of tinkering is the most productive way to fix anything that needs fixing.

Things to do and notice

These activities require the redesign and fabrication of new cars. The goal is to identify the parts of the design that have the greatest effect on performance.

- Experiment with the body shape to see what impact it has on car speed.

- Experiment with the wheel diameter to see how it affects car speed.

- Build several different propellers to see how car speed depends on propeller size and number of blades.

- Design a new car using two motor-driven propellers to let the car change direction.

- Instead of nails, what other materials can be used for the axles (e.g., coat hanger, wire, etc.)? Which axle material works best? Why is this?

6 – Tensegrity Models for Polyhedra

Design and build open-frame models of polyhedra using only compressive struts and tensile elements. This can be done completely using only Inkscape and OpenSCAD.

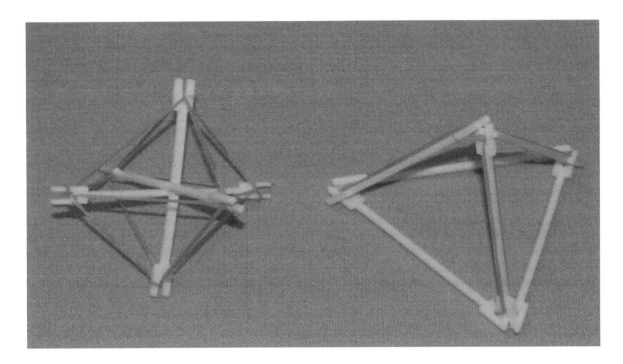

Background

Polyhedra are three-dimensional structures made with straight lines. All polyhedra have flat faces, straight edges and corners, sometimes called vertices. These geometric shapes are often explored in mathematics classes.

Our approach to exploring polyhedra is through the use of what are called tensegrity structures, first developed by Buckminster Fuller. Tensegrity, (a word he coined based on "tensional integrity") is a structural principle based on the use of isolated components in compression inside a net of continuous tension. In pure tensegrity structures, the compressed members (usually bars or struts) do not touch each other, and the tensioned members (usually cables or tendons) determine the overall structure of the space. In our models, the compressed members may touch each other, although they are usually free to slide against each other at the point where they touch.

Our models are made with plastic struts fabricated on the 3D printer, which are held together using rubber bands as the tension elements.

NGSS Areas

Disciplinary Core Idea(s)

- Engineering

How Scientists and Engineers Work

- Experimentation and problem-solving

CCSS Math Connections

- Make sense of problems and persevere in solving them.
- Reason abstractly and quantitatively.
- Construct viable arguments and critique the reasoning of others.
- Model with mathematics.
- Use appropriate tools strategically.
- Attend to precision.
- Look for and make use of structure.
- Look for and express regularity in repeated reasoning.

Materials

- Plastic struts made on the 3D printer
- Rubber bands (size 19 and 32) available from office supply stores

Construction details

1. Open Inkscape and create a rectangle 80 mm wide and 3 mm high.

2. Next, make another rectangle 15 mm wide and 8 mm high. This rectangle will be turned into a hook to hold the rubber bands.

3. Make an oval 15 mm wide and 4 mm high and overlap the oval with the large rectangle by a bit more than 50%.

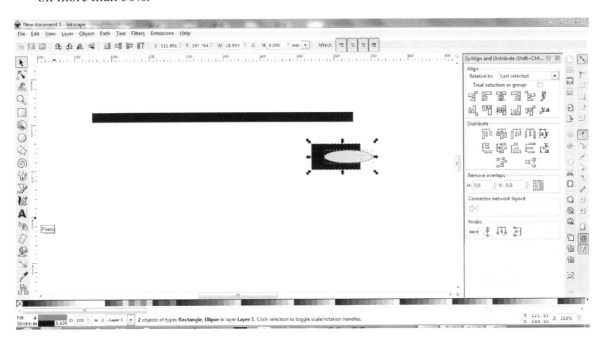

4. Select the oval and large rectangle and center vertically using the Align and Distribute tool in the Object menu. While these objects are still selected, choose Difference from the Path menu to cut out a region of the large rectangle.

5. Copy the large rectangle with the cutout in it, paste a copy, and flip copy left to right using the Flip horizontal tool in the line below the menu bar. This will give you two cutout pieces, one facing left, and the other facing right.

6. Save your work on the desktop as, for example, [struts.svg].

7. Next, position the cutout pieces over the left and right ends of the long rectangle so the cutouts do not overlap the horizontal line.

8. Select all three pieces and center vertically.

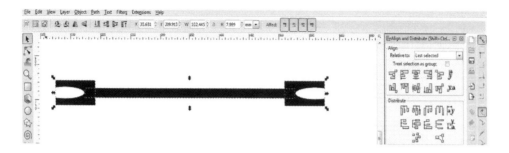

9. With all three parts selected, choose Group from the Object menu to lock all the pieces together.

10. Once this is done, save your work, and copy the finished strut, and paste copies to create eight struts. Leave a little space between adjacent struts to make them easy to separate when they are printed.

11. Select all eight struts. Align their left ends and distribute them from the centers top/bottom using the Align and Distribute tools in the Object menu.

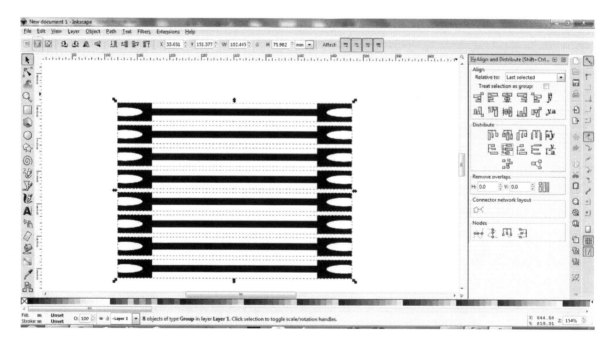

12. Next, select Paths to OpenSCAD from the Generate from Paths option under the Extension menu and extrude the completed drawing to 3 mm. Save this file on the desktop as [struts. scad] and save your Inkscape file again.

13. Open the [struts.scad] file in OpenSCAD and choose Compile and Render from the Design menu. Your image should look like this:

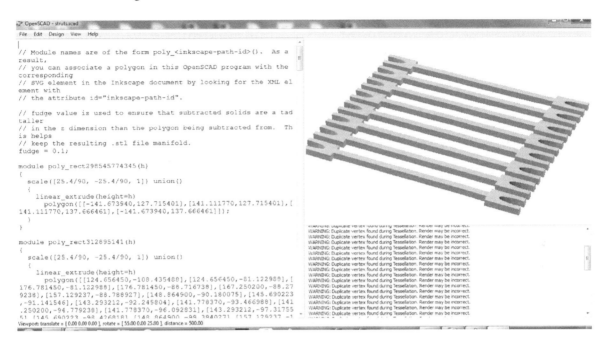

14. From the Design menu choose Export as STL and save the file on the desktop as [struts.stl]. Your design is now ready for printing.

15. Assemble polyhedra using struts and rubber bands. Experiment with rubber band sizes to find the right one that makes the finished model look nice.

Things to do and notice

Some of these activities may use a lot of struts, so you should build a few sets before starting. Some of these structures may take two sets of hands to assemble. Technically, the polyhedra you will be building are not pure tensegrity structures because the struts are touching.

- Using rubber bands and the struts you printed, build a few simple polyhedra – tetrahedron, octahedron, cube, etc.
- Note that the tetrahedron can only be made if the struts are along the edges. Why is this?
- Explore the relationship between the number of faces, edges, and corners of various polyhedra. You can use a spreadsheet to hold the data for each polyhedron.
- When you find the rule connecting these numbers, how can you prove that the result is true for all polyhedra?
- Do some research on pure tensegrity structures: one for which no struts touch each other. Can you build one of these structures using your struts and rubber bands?
- While edges and corners can easily be identified in these new structures, examine your structure to see what conclusions you can draw about the faces.

7 – Two-Gear Clock

Design and build a simple clock that only uses two 3D-printed gears.

Background

Mechanical timepieces have been around for many hundreds of years. The design and construction of a geared clock can be very complex, but it is possible to build simpler clocks like this one.

NGSS Areas

Disciplinary Core Idea(s):

- Physical Science
- Engineering
- Earth and Space Science
- How we measure time

How Scientists and Engineers Work:

- Tinkering and experimentation

Transferability:

- History
- Origins of mechanical clocks, etc.

CCSS Math Connections

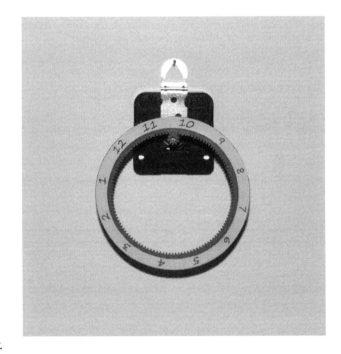

- Make sense of problems and persevere in solving them.
- Reason abstractly and quantitatively.
- Construct viable arguments and critique the reasoning of others.
- Model with mathematics.
- Use appropriate tools strategically.
- Attend to precision.
- Look for and make use of structure.

Materials

- Battery-operated clock motor from hobby store
- Glue stick

Construction details

1. Open Inkscape and create a gear with 120 teeth from the Render Gear command in the Extensions menu.

2. Create another gear with only 10 teeth. The ratio of the teeth is 12:1, so that for every rotation of the small gear, the large one turns by 1/12 that amount.

3. Place the small gear on the large one.

4. Select all, lock the width and height, and resize so the large gear has a diameter of 80 mm.

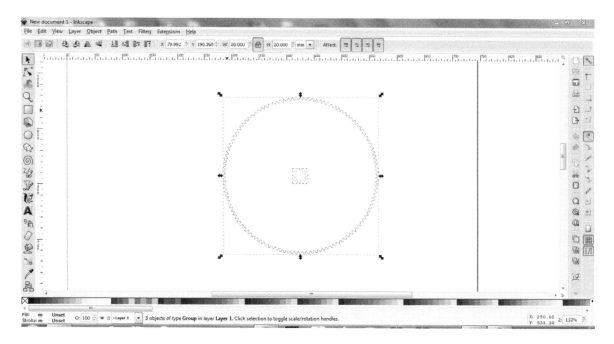

5. Draw a circle 100 mm in diameter. Select this object and lower to bottom from the Object menu.

6. Select both gears, and from the Object menu choose Ungroup.

7. Fill gears and the circle with different contrasting colors.

8. Drag the large gear over the circle.

9. Select the circle and the large gear and, from the Object menu, choose Align and Distribute, and center the circle and large gear vertically and horizontally.

10. With the large gear and circle selected, choose Difference in the Path menu to cut out the gear shape from the larger circle. This gives us a ring with the gear teeth on the inside.

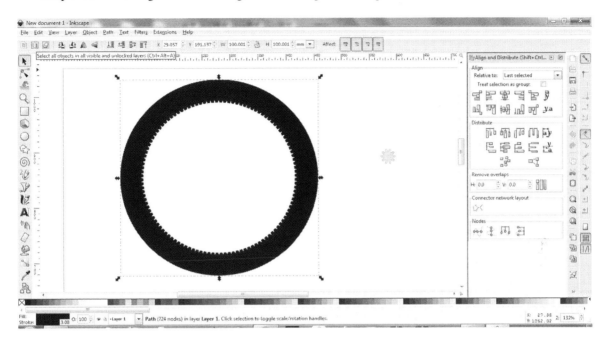

11. Using the same procedure, we next make a hole to fit the shaft of the clock motor. For the motor we used, we made the hole an oval 3.9 mm x 2.8 mm.

12. Place this hole artwork over the small gear, and select both.

13. From the Object menu, choose Align and Distribute, and center the hole both horizontally and vertically.

14. With both these objects selected, from the Path menu choose Difference to cut out the center hole from the small circle.

15. Save your work (e.g., [clock.svg]).

16. Select everything and from the Extensions menu, use the Paths to OpenSCAD command in Generate from Paths, and extrude the drawing by 3mm.

17. Save the file to the desktop as [clock.scad].

18. Open the scad file and from the Design menu, choose Compile and Render to see the finished shapes.

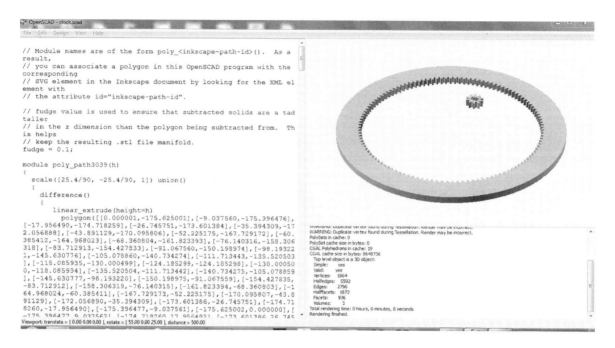

19. From the Design menu, export the drawing as an STL file (e.g., [clock.stl]).

20. Print the parts on your 3D printer.

21. Using Inkscape or another graphics program, design and print hour numbers for the large gear. Note these numbers run counterclockwise, because the small gear moves in the same direction as the large one.

22. Cut out and paste the "clock face" on the large gear with a glue stick.

23. Place the small gear on the "minutes" shaft of the clock motor so it rotates once per hour.

24. Hang your clock on the wall and set the large gear ring on the small gear so the current time is at the top of the ring.

Things to do and notice

Once the clock is built, you should hang it on a wall. The small gear only rotates once per hour, so you will need to be patient to see any movement. The following activities are based on the clock you just built.

- When you look at the clock, the numbers seem backwards from what you'd expect. How did the definition of "clockwise" evolve?

- How can the design be modified to keep the large ring from slipping off the small gear without obscuring the numbers?

- The two gears are quite different in that one has the teeth on the outside and the other has teeth on the inside of a ring. Do the two gears mesh properly? Can the design be changed to make the teeth mesh better?

8 – Pentagonal Tiles

Design and build a set of simple tiles that incorporate regular pentagons.

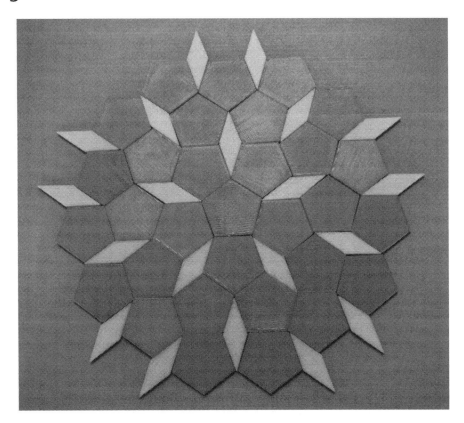

Background

Unlike triangles, quadrilaterals, and hexagons, you cannot tile a surface with regular pentagons alone. However, if you add a parallelogram to the set, you can create many interesting tiling patterns, some that look like Penrose tilings.

Penrose tiling is a geometrical pattern generated by special tiles that expand from a central point but cannot be replicated on a grid. A shifted copy of a Penrose tiling will never match the original. Unlike traditional tiling patterns made with (for example) triangles, quadrilaterals, and hexagons,

Penrose tiles can show five-fold rotational symmetry (as can some of the patterns made with tiles created in this project).

In this project we will create two shapes of tiles – regular pentagons and diamonds – that can be used to build tiling patterns of different symmetries, some of which can grow forever, and others that stop growing after reaching a certain point.

NGSS Areas

How Scientists and Engineers Work:

- Tinkering and experimentation

CCSS Math Connections

- Make sense of problems and persevere in solving them.
- Reason abstractly and quantitatively.
- Model with mathematics.
- Use appropriate tools strategically.
- Attend to precision.
- Look for and make use of structure.

Construction details

1. Open Inkscape and create a regular pentagon by clicking on the polygon tool in the left toolbar. This brings up a special menu beneath the main menu bar.

2. Click the polygon button, choose 5 corners, and draw a pentagon on the screen. Rotate this pentagon so one side is horizontal.

3. Next, select the pentagon and click the lock icon next to the width setting window (W).

4. Set the width to 30 mm.

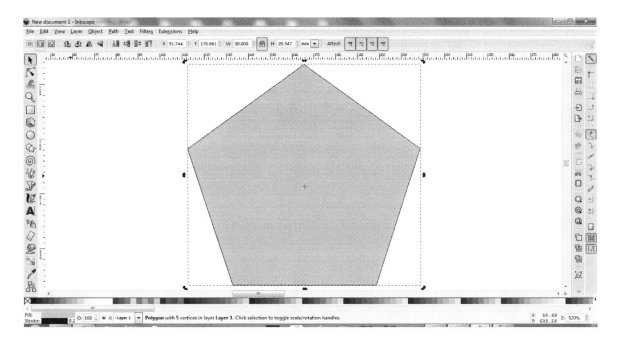

5. Copy this pentagon and paste a copy on the screen.

6. With the copy selected, flip the pentagon vertically using the flip tool below the main menu, and align the flipped copy so the horizontal line of the copy touches the horizontal line of the first pentagon.

7. Paste another copy of the pentagon on the screen and move it so its edge aligns with the lower right edge of the original pentagon.

8. Next, copy the lower left polygon and paste and move copies so they fit properly on the edges of the pentagons on the right side.

9. Save your work (for example, [pentagons.svg]).

10. The diamond shape is the next tile piece we need. This represents the only other shape we need to make simple patterns that also use regular pentagons. To make this shape, choose the Draw Bezier curves and straight lines tool from the left vertical menu bar and click four points to draw a quadrilateral. It is important that the last point perfectly overlaps the starting point. Fill this quadrilateral with a different color, select this shape and, using the Edit paths by nodes tool in the left vertical menu bar, carefully drag each corner (shaded grey) to one of the corners of the diamond shape in the pentagonal pattern. This completes the basic shapes we will use.

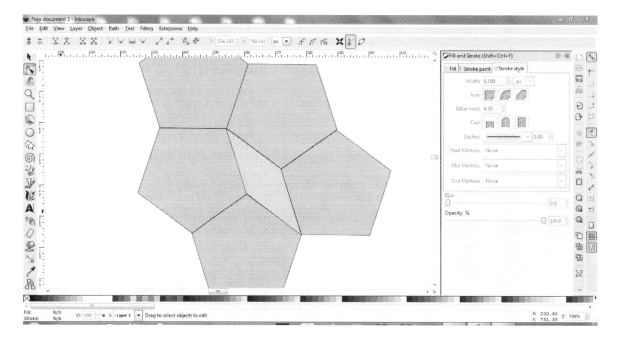

11. Save your work.

12. Select one of the pentagons, copy it, and paste the copy in a new Inkscape page.

13. Paste several pentagons and align and distribute them into a pattern with enough gaps to make them easy to separate when printed. Keep the gaps fairly small to be sure the whole set of tiles fits on the platform of your printer. Depending on your printer, you might want to use fewer pentagons in your drawing.

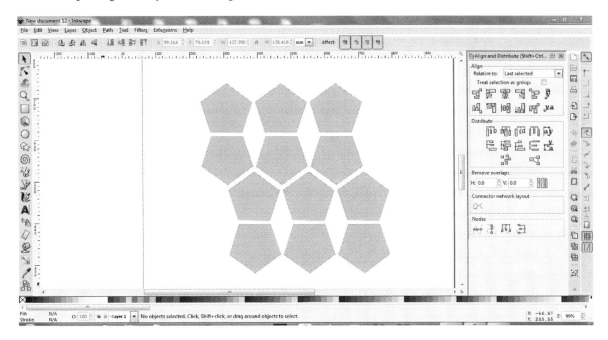

14. Save this drawing (e.g., [tile1.svg]).

15. Select everything and from the Extensions menu, use the Paths to OpenSCAD command in Generate from Paths, and extrude the drawing by 2.5 mm.

16. Save the file to the desktop as [tile1.scad].

17. Open the scad file and from the Design menu, choose Compile and Render to see the finished shapes.

18. From the Design menu, export the drawing as an STL file (e.g., [tile1.stl]).

19. Print the parts on your 3D printer. You may want to make about 50 of these tiles.

20. Repeat this process with the diamond shapes by pasting a copy in a new Inkscape document, and pasting copies into a nice pattern for printing that leaves enough room between the tiles so they can be separated easily.

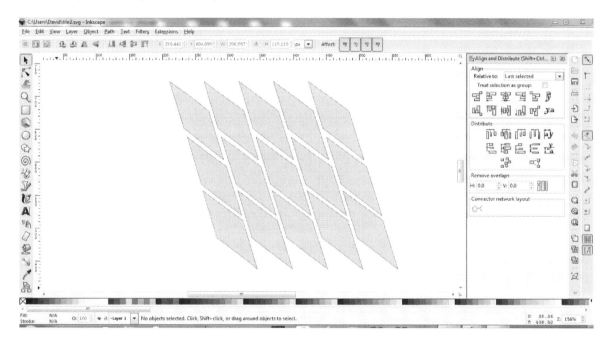

21. Save this drawing (e.g., [tile2.svg]).

22. Select everything and from the Extensions menu, use the Paths to OpenSCAD command in Generate from Paths, and extrude the drawing by 2.5 mm.

23. Save the file to the desktop as [tile2.scad].

24. Open the scad file and from the Design menu, choose Compile and Render to see the finished shapes.

25. From the Design menu export the drawing as an STL file (e.g., [tile2.stl]).

26. Print at least two sets of these parts on your 3D printer. You may want to use a different color for these tiles so they contrast nicely with the pentagons.

Things to do and notice

These activities make use of the tiles you just created. You should make lots of tiles to work with. You might want to make about a hundred of each tile so you can see how patterns emerge as you experiment with different configurations.

- Experiment with different tiling patterns that cover a flat surface without leaving any gaps. What do you notice about the patterns you create? Does your pattern allow you to tile a floor?

- Explore the construction of a tiling pattern starting with a pentagon in the center. Can you build a pattern that has five-fold rotational symmetry? Is this pattern better or worse for tiling a floor?

- Can you create a tiling pattern that has neither rotational nor translational symmetry, but still could be used to tile a floor?

- What is the smallest repeating tiling pattern you can find?

- Does every pattern have the same ratio of diamond tiles to pentagonal tiles? Build a spreadsheet with the numbers entered for each pattern you create.

- How many tiling patterns can you find that use both tiles?

9 – Pentagrams

Make five-pointed stars (pentagrams) to work with the previous project on pentagonal tiling.

Background

The previous project showed that interesting tiling patterns can be made using regular pentagons and diamond-shaped tiles. In this project we build pentagrams that, when added to the previous set, allow the creation of different tiling patterns. The resulting patterns have different symmetries than the kind demonstrated with the original two shapes.

NGSS Areas

How Scientists and Engineers Work:

- Tinkering and experimentation

CCSS Math Connections

- Make sense of problems and persevere in solving them.
- Reason abstractly and quantitatively.
- Model with mathematics.
- Use appropriate tools strategically.
- Attend to precision.
- Look for and make use of structure.

Construction details

1. Open the Inkscape file with the final pentagons from the previous project ([tile1.svg] is the name we gave this file).

2. Copy one of the pentagons that has the point on top and paste it into a new Inkscape file.

3. Add four more copies to create the pattern shown below. Be sure to position the pentagons accurately with the points touching perfectly.

4. Select the polygon tool from the left side vertical menu bar.

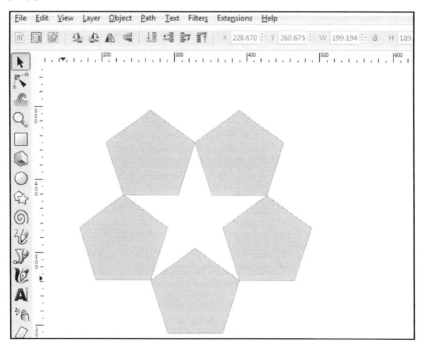

5. At the top menu, choose 5 for the number of sides, and choose the star shape.

6. Draw a five-pointed star inside the central opening of the pentagonal pattern – don't worry of it doesn't fit exactly, but be sure it is aligned properly so the point is at the very top. Fill this shape with a color of your choice.

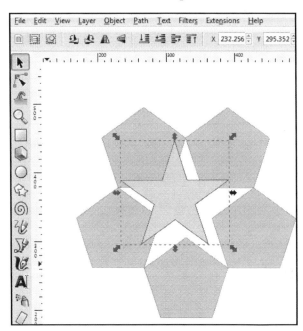

7. Select the pentagram (the star) and, to maintain the aspect ratio when you change the size, click on the little lock between the width and height boxes at the top of the screen.

8. Pull the corner of the selected star to reach the right size, and move the star inside the pentagonal pattern to be sure the edges and arm lengths are exactly right. This may take some effort to get right, but the results will be worth it.

9. Save your work (for example, [star.svg]).

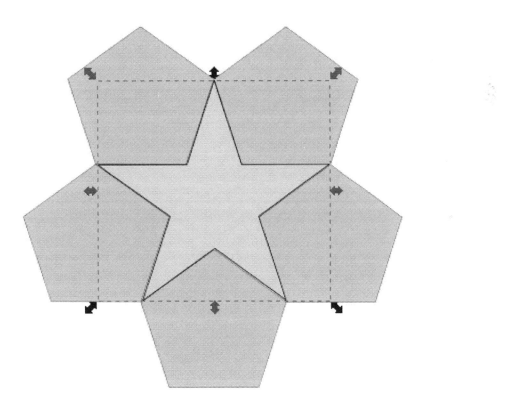

10. Copy the star shape and open a new Inkscape window. Paste copies of the star so several of them can be printed at once. Depending on the size of your printer's platform, you might be able to print six at once. Be sure to leave enough space between the stars to make it easy to separate them after printing.

11. Save this drawing as [tile3.svg], for example.

12. Select everything and from the Extensions menu, use the Paths to OpenSCAD command in Generate from Paths, and extrude the drawing by 2.5 mm.

13. Save the file to the desktop as [tile1.scad].

14. Open the scad file and from the Design menu choose Compile and Render to see the finished shapes.

15. From the Design menu export the drawing as an STL file (e.g., [tile1.stl]).

16. Print the parts on your 3D printer. You may want to make about 12 of these tiles.

17. Add these tiles to the others you made in the previous project so you can make patterns using all three shapes.

Things to do and notice

These activities make use of the tiles you just created, mixed with the tiles from the previous set. Depending on your interest, you should make lots of tiles to work with. You might want to make about a hundred of each tile so you can see how patterns emerge as you experiment with different configurations.

- Using all three tiles, experiment with different tiling patterns that cover a flat surface without leaving any gaps. What do you notice about the patterns you create? Does your pattern allow you to tile a floor?

- Explore the construction of a tiling pattern starting with a star in the center. Can you build a pattern that has five-fold rotational symmetry? Why or why not? Is this pattern better or worse for tiling a floor?

- What is the smallest repeating tiling pattern you can find?

- Does every pattern have the same ratio of diamond tiles to pentagonal tiles? Build a spreadsheet with the numbers entered for each pattern you create.

- How many tiling patterns can you find that use all three tiles?

- Play a two-player game where you start with a star in the center and players take turns adding to the pattern. Each player's points for each turn are made by counting the number of edges the new tile shares with the existing pattern. Play continues until you either run out of tiles, or there is no place to add any more with the shapes you have. The player with the most points wins.

10 – Exploring Knots

Design and build mathematical knots of different complexity.

Background

This project is the most abstract one in this book. It deals with a branch of mathematics called "Knot Theory." The results of this exploration can be quite beautiful, and this project helps kids see the real beauty of mathematics.

Anyone who has tied a ribbon on a package or tied a shoe knows something about knots. In both cases, it is usual to make two knots – a simple overhand knot, and a bow knot on top. The bow can be untied by simply pulling on the two strands from which the knot was tied. While very useful, the bow is not actually a knot because it can be undone just by pulling the ends.

Mathematically, Knot Theory is a branch of topology. The simplest form of Knot Theory involves the embedding of the unit circle into three-dimensional space. A mathematical knot is somewhat different from the usual idea of a knot, that is, a piece of string with free ends. The knots studied in Knot Theory are (almost) always considered to be closed loops. If the loop can be untangled to create an open shape like a circle, the starting structure is not a knot. If, however, there is no way to untie the shape, then it is a real knot, and there are many hundreds of them. Anyone interested in knowing more about Knot Theory is advised to visit the KnotPlot site (www.knotplot.com) and read some of the materials posted there.

Our goal with this project is to show that 3D printing has a role to play in abstract mathematics, sometimes allowing the creation of beautiful artifacts. The software we will employ can be used by just about anyone interesting in tinkering with some amazing 3D patterns, any of which can be printed if you like.

NGSS Areas

Disciplinary Core Idea(s):

- Engineering

How Scientists and Engineers Work:

- Tinkering and experimentation

CCSS Math Connections

- Make sense of problems and persevere in solving them.
- Reason abstractly and quantitatively.
- Construct viable arguments and critique the reasoning of others.
- Model with mathematics.
- Use appropriate tools strategically.
- Attend to precision.
- Look for and make use of structure.
- Look for and express regularity in repeated reasoning.

Construction details

1. Install KnotPlot.

2. Create a folder on your desktop (call it Knots). This folder will have a shortcut to the program and also be the place where completed knot files are stored. In order to set this up, edit the "Start in:" properties of your shortcut icon to provide the full path to your folder. In our case, this path is C:\users\david\desktop\knotplot. (By the way, Mac users don't have to deal with all this – just follow the directions in the "Read Me" file when you install Knotplot.) We know this seems complex, but all we can say is that this is really worth the effort (as we shall soon see).

3. Launch KnotPlot. This will put four windows on your screen, two for text, one for the graphic of your knots, and one with buttons to open knots, manipulate them, and export them as STL files so you can print them. Because we will not need the text windows, just be sure the graphic and control button windows are on the top and next to each other. While KnotPlot is capable of doing many more things in the text windows than those represented by the button window, this is all you need for our project. If, when we are done, you are hooked and want to dig deeper, be our guest!

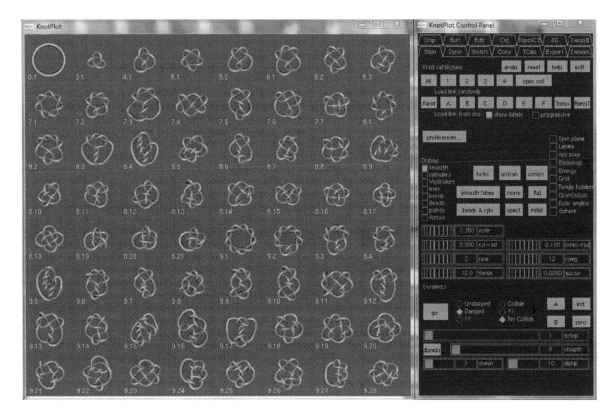

4. This image shows one page (of many) of the kinds of knots that are built-in to the software. Experiment with different buttons (labeled A, B, C, etc.) to see other libraries of images.

5. When you find one you like, click on the image in the graphic window and the knot will appear on the screen.

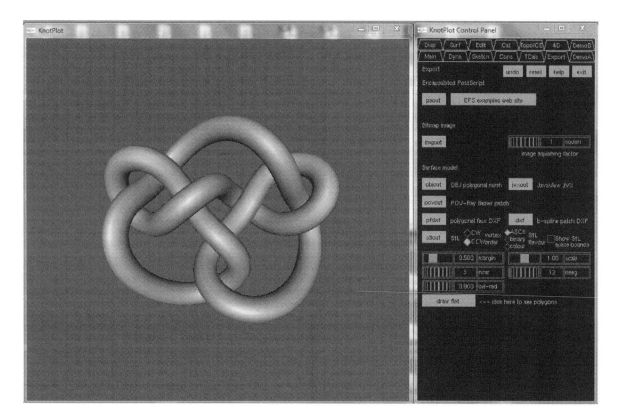

6. Once you find a knot you want to make on your printer, click on the Export tab on the button panel and then click on the STLOUT button under the Surface Model label, and your knot will be saved as [knot.stl] in the same folder that has your shortcut to KnotPlot (assuming you set everything up properly).

7. Rename this STL file so it doesn't get overwritten by the next knot you make.

8. When you decide the print your knot, you may find that the model is pretty small and could be wider. To fix this, your 3D printer software has a scale command that lets you expand or shrink a model to make it fit. You want to apply this command to all three dimensions and position the final model on the stage properly so it can be printed. The following image shows what this looks like for the Afinia printer we use. We scaled the image up by a factor of 3 so the model would be larger and easier to manipulate.

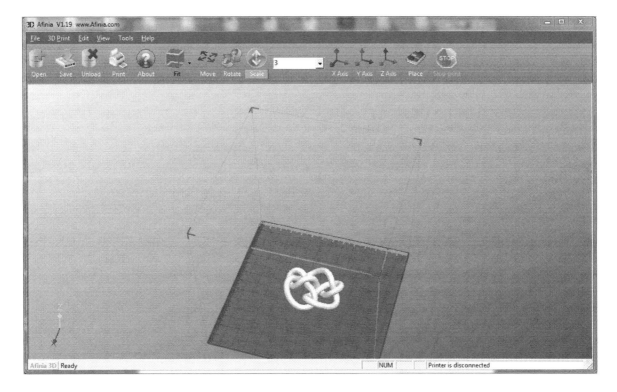

9. If you are making knot sculptures to use as jewelry, you might be happy with a pendant the original size, or you might even want to shrink it a bit – the choice is yours.

10. On the topic of jewelry, as we mentioned earlier in this book, there are services that will gladly plate your plastic model in nickel, copper, or bronze (www.repliforminc.com/RePliKote.htm). Also, you can send your file to Shapeways (www.shapeways.com) and they will not only make it, but provide you with the option to make your model with precious metals.

Things to do and notice

- After printing a knot, turn it around in your hand and see if there are paths that let you see straight through the loops. If so, what do these loops say about the complexity of the knot?

- Knots that are connected together with extra parts are called links, and there are models for some of these that you might find interesting.

- Using the editing tools in KnotPlot, can you design and print a knot of your own?

11 – Designing Creatures

Sculpt creatures of your own design.

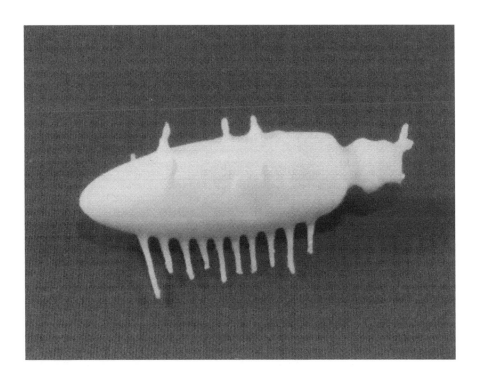

Background

So far all the projects in this book have been built from geometric shapes. This project breaks that mold. Instead of drawing objects to print, we will sculpt them with a 3D modeling tool that resembles working with clay. Don't worry if your artistic skills aren't very high. If you ever worked with Play Doh™ or modeling clay, you will get the hang of these new tools very quickly.

We will design an imaginary but fanciful insect, but you are encouraged to create anything you want.

NGSS Areas

Disciplinary Core Idea(s):

- Life Sciences

How scientists and engineers work:

- Tinkering and experimentation

CCSS Math Connections

- Use appropriate tools strategically.
- Attend to precision.
- Look for and make use of structure.

Construction details

1. Install and launch Meshmixer. You will start with a blank screen. Start by importing a sphere (although you could import any 3D drawing you have handy).

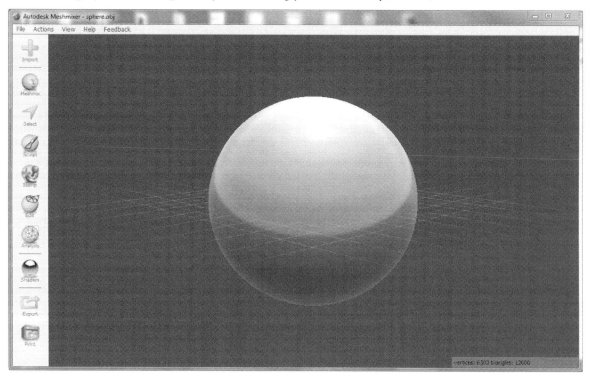

2. Because we are building a "living thing" with lots of symmetry in it, click the "symmetry" button found when you choose the sculpt tool. This will draw a white line around the center of the object so that any change you make to the left side of the drawing appears on the right side as well. This not only saves a lot of time, it makes your creatures look more real.

3. Next click on the "edit mesh" button on the left and choose "transform." Our goal here is to squish the sphere into a thinner and longer oval shape. To rotate your shape, hold the "alt" key and the left mouse button. As you move the mouse, the shape will rotate to different orientations. Once you have the axes aligned the way you want, drag the arrows to make the vertical (z) axis smaller, and the depth (y) axis longer.

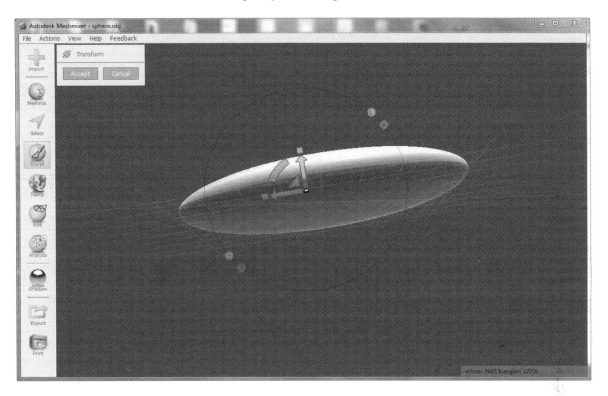

4. Once this is done, you can start adding details to the shape using the sculpting tools. You should experiment with various tools to see what they do. You will want to adjust your view so the action of the tools can be seen. If you make any mistakes, just press Ctrl-Z and you will undo the last action. If you want, you can keep doing this until you get back to the original sphere.

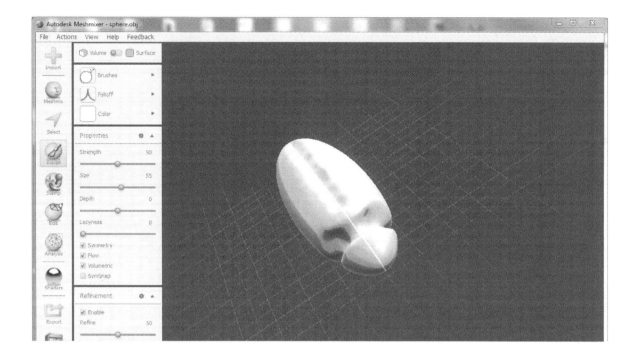

5. As you work on your project, save your file frequently. The saved files can only be opened in Meshmixer. When you are done, you can export your finished model to an STL file.

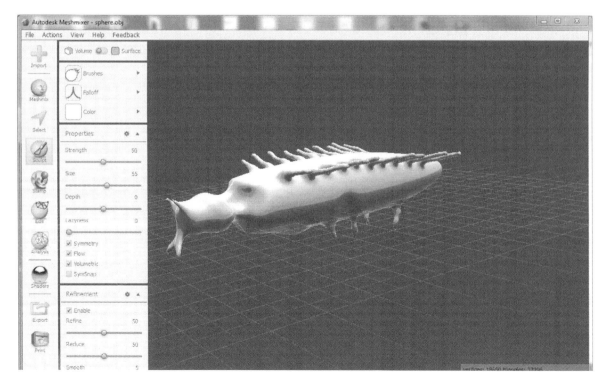

6. Once your model is finished, export it as an STL file and print it out. You may find that your printer has to add a lot of supporting structures so the legs and other parts print properly. Be very careful in removing these parts so the fine details of your model don't break off!

Things to do and notice

- The creature we designed has left-right symmetry. Does this symmetry exist for all animals? What advantages do animals have if they are symmetric?

- The gravitational force on the Moon and Mars is lower than what we experience on Earth. How would animals on different planets be influenced by the gravitational force they experience?

- Would animals from one planet be able to live on another one if the gravitational pull there is greater?

- Instead of Meshmixer, try the Sculptris software to decide which you like better.

12 – Printing Your Own Fossils

Using resources from several museums, build and explore 3D models of fossils.

Background

Earlier in this book we cautioned against relying on Thingiverse as the source of objects that students would simply print. This project involves downloading a certain type of 3D model to build, and then to explore – Fossils. The reason for bending our suggestion in this case is because the physical inspection of accurate fossil models is something most kids never get to do. Museums have these priceless artifacts behind glass, and there is so much that can be learned by holding these shapes in your hands, even if they are only plastic models.

Museums that are in the process of digitizing their collection include the Smithsonian in Washington, DC (3d.si.edu) and the African fossils collection (africanfossils.org). The scanned collections from that museum include specimens housed in the National Museums of Kenya and the Turkana Basin Institute field stations.

The Museum Victoria (Melbourne, Australia) collection takes a different approach to image distribution. Rather than make the STL files of artifacts available from their website they have posted them on Thingiverse (www.thingiverse.com). At this time they have two models posted – an Ammonite and a Trilobite.

It is only a matter of time before more museums make artifacts based on their collections available in this way, so keep looking!

Each institution has employed several methods for building models, ranging from CT scans to laser scanning or even making 3D photographs of the objects. No matter what scanning method is chosen, the goal is the same: to create accurate models that can be fabricated on a 3D printer.

NGSS Areas

Disciplinary Core Idea(s):

- Life Sciences
- Engineering

CCSS Math Connections

- Look for and make use of structure.
- Look for and express regularity in repeated reasoning.

Construction details

1. Download the MuseumVictoria Ammonite model from Thingiverse (goo.gl/RPz4ir).

2. Open the model in Meshlab. This lets you see what you are going to print, and also cleans the model of extraneous components without changing the quality of the fossil at all.

3. As you rotate the model in Meshlab, you see that it appears to be a spiral shell with grooves on both sides.

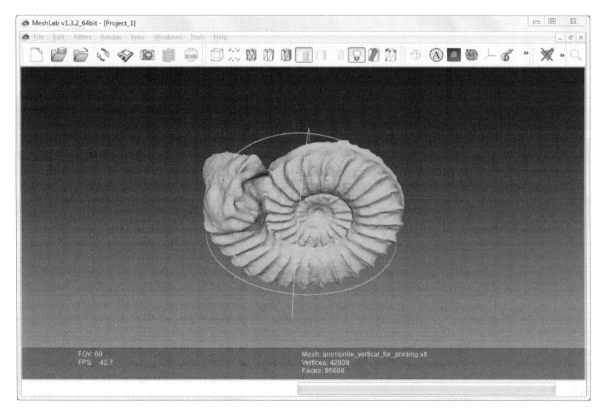

4. Print your model in a color like white or brown to make the "fossil" look more real.

Things to do and notice

- This artifact appears to be a shell of some kind. What kind of animal would live in this shell?
- Measure the spiral pattern to see if it is similar to the shells of animals living today.
- What can you find about Ammonites by searching on the web (Wikipedia, for example)?
- Why did the Ammonite become extinct?

13 – Designing a Mobile Sculpture

Design and build a kinetic sculpture in the spirit of Alexander Calder.

Background

Alexander Calder was an American sculptor who worked in the early to mid-20th Century. He is best known as the originator of the mobile, a type of kinetic sculpture made with delicately balanced or suspended components which move in response to motor power or air currents. His work on this kind of sculpture became so well known, that the word "mobile" triggers his name wherever they are spoken of or seen, even though other artists have built (and are building) kinetic sculptures of their own. Calder did a lot of his work in France, and his beautiful pieces can been seen all over the world.

The basic structure of his pieces consists of several vanes that are held together with long strands of thin wire. The vanes catch breezes, causing the sculpture to move – often creating interesting arrangements by chance.

NGSS Areas

Disciplinary Core Idea(s):

- Engineering

How Scientists and Engineers Work:

- Tinkering and experimentation

CCSS Math Connections

- Use appropriate tools strategically.
- Look for and make use of structure.

Construction details

1. Open Inkscape and draw two circles, one 30 mm in diameter, and the other 10 mm in diameter.

2. Using the "Draw Bezier curves and straight lines" tool on the left vertical bar (the tool two up from the text tool), draw a quadrilateral as shown below, making sure the ending point is the same as the starting point.

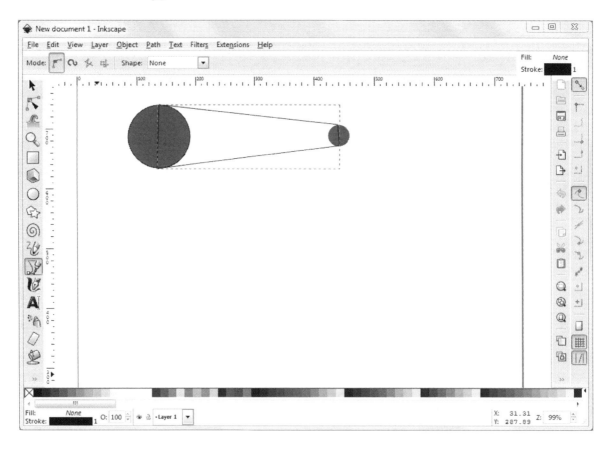

3. Next choose the narrow selection arrow in the left toolbar – this is the one just below the main selection tool called "Edit paths by nodes." It allows you to bend the lines you have just drawn.

4. First, using this tool, click on the top line a bit to the left of center and, with the mouse button held down, move the mouse up to give a nice curved line.

5. Repeat this process for the bottom line so you have something similar to the shape shown below.

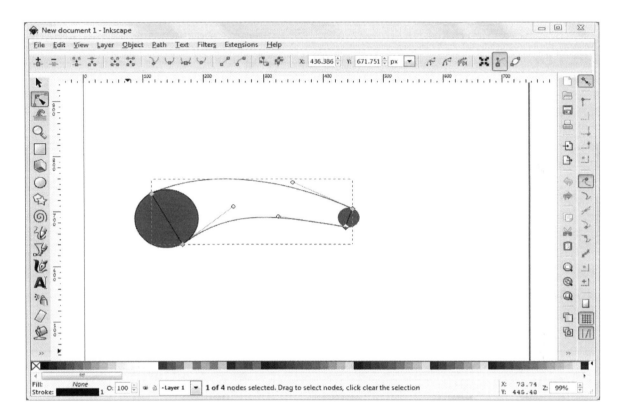

6. Next, before leaving this tool, adjust the four square diamonds at the corners of the shape so they make lines tangent to the circle.

7. Fill the open shape with the same color as the circles to complete the basic shape.

8. Select the entire shape (group it if you like), and adjust its horizontal dimension to 100 mm. Be sure the "lock" is on for the resizing process so you don't change the aspect ratio.

9. Copy the main shape and paste three copies on the screen.

10. Resize one of them to 50 mm wide, and the other two to 25 mm wide.

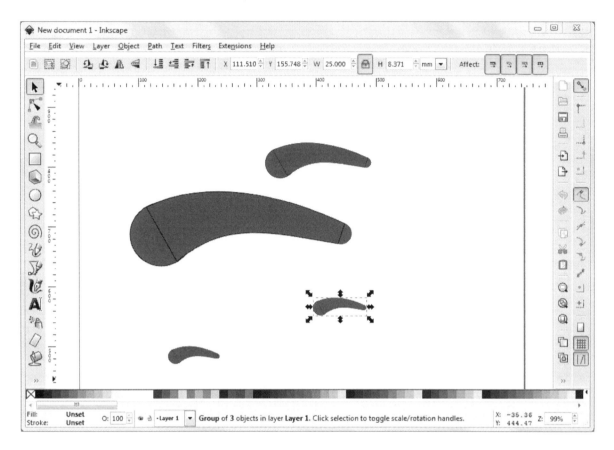

11. Now we need to put three small holes in each shape. To do this, be sure that each of the four shapes is ungrouped.

12. Draw a circle with a diameter of 1.5 mm and fill it with a different color.

13. Paste copies of this circle on each of the shapes pretty much where we have placed them. These circles will become holes in the finished parts.

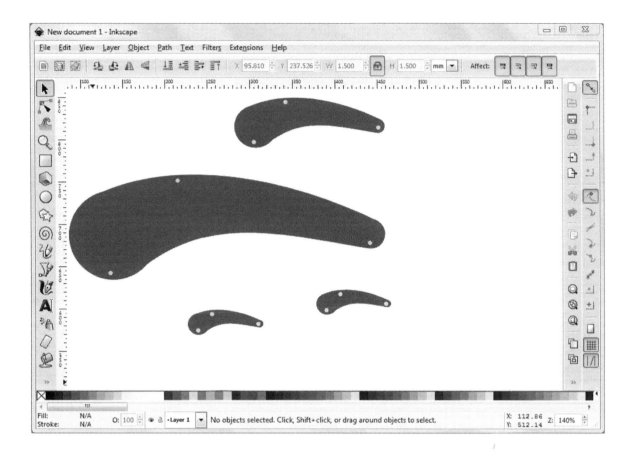

14. Save your work!

15. For each shape, select a circle and the object directly beneath it (a circle or the arced shape).

16. Using the Difference tool in the Paths menu, your small circle will become a hole.

17. Repeat this process for the remaining holes.

18. You have now finished the basic arm pieces for your mobile, so save your work!

19. It is time to extrude the parts into shapes your 3D printer can make. To do this, select all the parts (Ctrl-A) and from the Extensions menu, choose Generate from Path, and Paths to OpenSCAD. If everything works, you will see a window open that will let you add thickness to your parts. Choose the thickness you want – 2.5mm, for example, and then choose an output file name such as [~/desktop/mobilebase.scad] and click Apply, and then Done. This will generate a file you can open in OpenSCAD.

20. Open the OpenSCAD file you just created. Go to the Design menu and choose Compile and Render (F6). Your finished shapes will now show up as a 3D object you can rotate with your mouse to examine from different angles.

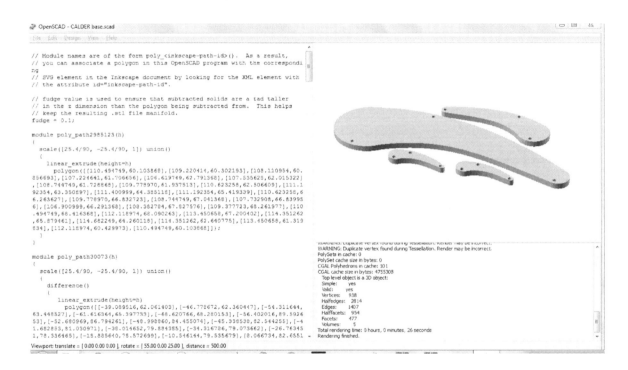

21. Now go to the Design menu and choose Export as STL, and save the file on your desktop where it is easy to find, [mobile arms.stl], for example.

22. While not necessary, you can clean up the file from extraneous complexity by opening the STL file in Meshlab, letting it clean the image, and then saving it again for printing. This step is not needed, but it never hurts!

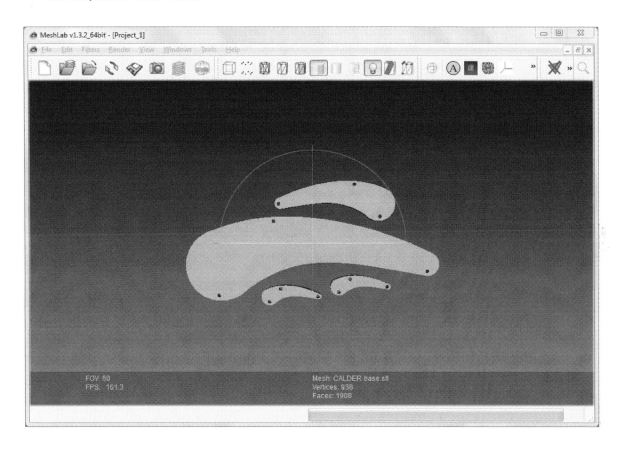

23. Go back to your original Inkscape file and add more shapes you can hang on your mobile.

24. Be sure to put small holes near the tops of each shape.

25. Select these shapes and export them to OpenSCAD so they can be compiled and turned into another STL file you can print. You can use a different thickness (2 mm) if you wish.

26. Print your shapes.

27. To assemble your mobile, use thread to connect the pieces together, with the small objects at the bottom. Start with the largest piece at the top, and work down from there.

28. When you are done, tie a thread from the top hole in the large piece from which the mobile can be hung. If you don't like the arrangement you have chosen, try other ones.

Things to do and notice

- Depending on where you placed the holes in the arms, your sculpture might not balance properly. How can you decide exactly where the top holes should be placed?

- If you do change the hole positions, will the changes be the same for each of the arms?

- Experiment with different designs for your sculpture. For example, can you design one that can be used as a crib toy for a baby?

14 – Making Escher-Style Tiles

Design and build tiles in the style of tessellations by the artist M. C. Escher.

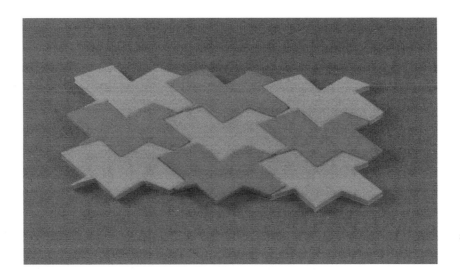

Background

The mathematically inspired woodcuts and lithographs of the Dutch artist M.C. Escher have enchanted people for many years. Among his popular topics are tessellations, some of which deal with many beautiful mathematical concepts. For example, his 1950's piece, Circle Limit III (shown in the Wikipedia entry at en.wikipedia.org/wiki/M_c_escher), is quite engaging. For those just starting out, his patterns are too complex for us to replicate as 3D tile pieces, but you will create some Escher-like tiles of your own design that can be used to tile a surface.

NGSS Areas

Disciplinary Core Idea(s):
- Engineering

How Scientists and Engineers Work:
- Tinkering and experimentation

CCSS Math Connections

- Make sense of problems and persevere in solving them.
- Reason abstractly and quantitatively.
- Use appropriate tools strategically.
- Attend to precision.
- Look for and make use of structure.
- Look for and express regularity in repeated reasoning.

Construction details

1. This project will use SketchUp Make, so install that program.

2. When you open SketchUp, you need to choose a template. For our work, choose the 3D Printing – Millimeters template.

3. From the Extensions Warehouse under the Windows menu, install the SketchUp STL extension so you will be able to export tiles that can be made on your printer. Sketchup is now ready to use.

4. Select the "Makerbot" box with your mouse and press the Delete key to remove it.

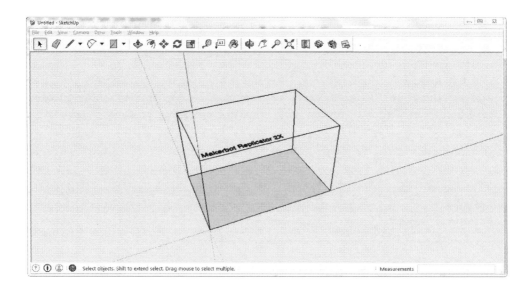

5. Choose Top from Standards Views in the Camera menu so you are looking straight down on the workspace.

6. Uncheck Perspective from the Camera menu

7. Draw a rectangle with the shapes tool below the menu bar (it looks like a rectangle with a line drawn through it). Don't worry about the size at this point.

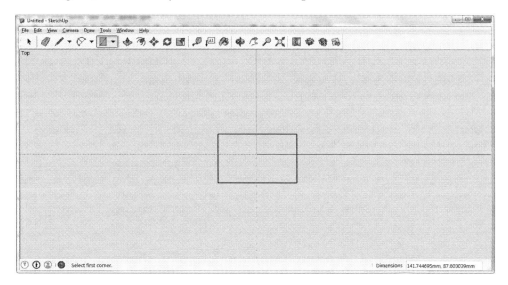

8. Next, using the pencil tool, draw several connected straight line segments along the top line.

9. Next, using the black arrow selection tool at the left under the menu bar, select all the triangular shapes you created. You can do this by shift-clicking on each shape.

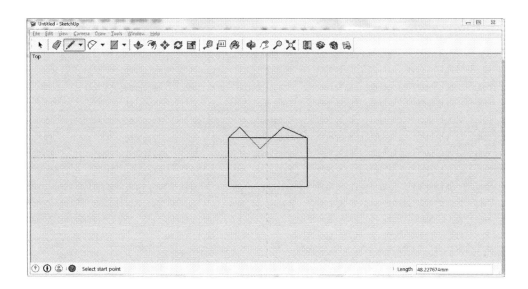

10. Next, click on the move tool (the one with the four red arrows) and move the cursor to the left top endpoint of the rectangle (a message will show when you are there. Press the Ctrl key and the left mouse button and drag the mouse down to the lower left endpoint. This moves a copy of the selected triangles to the bottom of the rectangle.

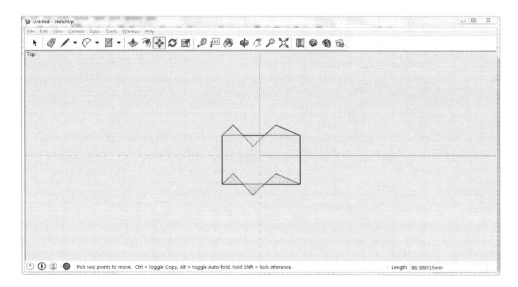

11. Repeat this process with other shapes on the right edge of the rectangle that you then select and move a copy to the left edge of the pattern.

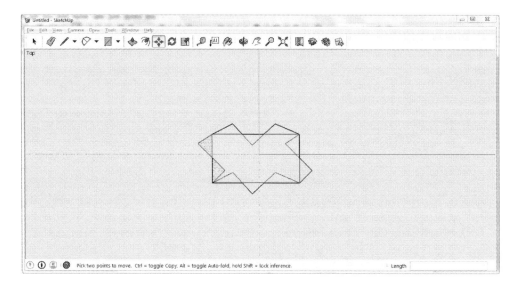

12. Next, use the eraser to click on all the original rectangle lines, leaving you with your new shape.

13. This strange shape might look like a fanciful bird. Don't worry about what it looks like at this point – you will get better with practice (pencil sketches help). What we need to do now is confirm that this shape will tile a surface.

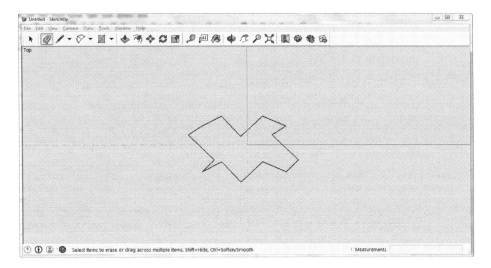

14. Before we make copies, let's give this shape some thickness so it will be a nice plastic tile when you build it. Using the ruler tool below the menu bar, we see that our shape is too big to print – in our case, about 160 mm. We need to scale it down by a bit so we can print a few of them at a time. Scaling by a factor of 4 should work fine.

15. To do this, select the tile and choose the scaling tool just to the left of the ruler. This puts some green dots around the shape. Drag the upper right dot toward the center of the shape until it is scaled to 0.25 times the original size.

16. At this point the shape is too small to work with, so click on the magnifying glass with the three red arrows to make the shape fill the screen.

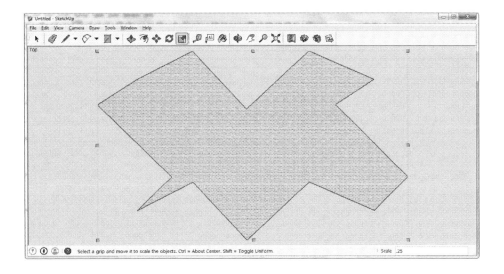

17. Now we are ready to add height to our tile. The first step is to select Iso from the Standard Views entry in the Camera menu.

18. Select the tile and then select the Push Pull tool. It looks like a square with an arrow coming out of the face. Click the mouse at one of the points on the shape and move the mouse up until the Distance (shown at the lower right of the screen) is 4 mm. To get the height exactly, just type 4 mm in the window next to the word Distance and the height will be set exactly.

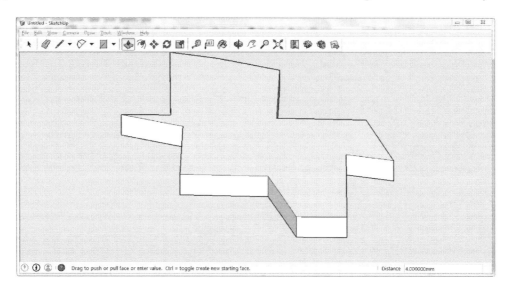

19. Next, select the entire tile by pressing Ctrl-A and turn it into a component by pressing the G key. This makes sure all parts stay attached as we copy and move our tile.

20. Save your work!

21. Now you are done, but you might want to be sure your tile "works." (It will, but don't take our word for it!)

22. Go back to the top view of the camera and use the regular magnifying glass to shrink your tile down in size so you will be able to put several of them on the screen.

23. Select the tile (this will put a rectangle around it because we turned it into a component).

24. Using the move tool, move the mouse to a left endpoint of the shape and hold the Ctrl key and left mouse button to drag a copy to the endpoint on the right side to put the copy in place. If you want more copies, enter (for example) 4x in the lower right window, and these copies will be made automatically.

25. Use the Pan tool (looks like a hand) to shift the view so you can see all the tiles.

26. Repeat the copying process vertically to build your pattern.

27. Using the Paint Bucket tool, color every other tile with a contrasting color. As you see, the tile you made "works" in that it fills space perfectly.

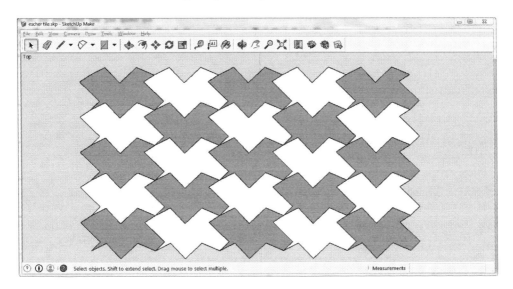

28. Now you are ready to export your tiles so they can be printed.

29. Erase all but 6 tiles and, using the Move tool, separate them so they can be easily separated when printed.

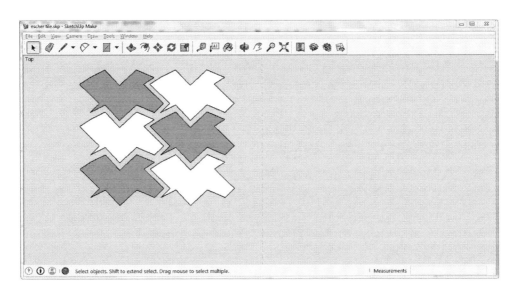

30. Choose Export to STL from the File menu. If this doesn't work, choose the OBJ option from the 3D Model entry in the Export menu item in the File menu.

31. If you choose this option, open the OBJ file in Meshlab. Ignore the warnings about color and you will see your tiles on the screen where you can look at them from different directions.

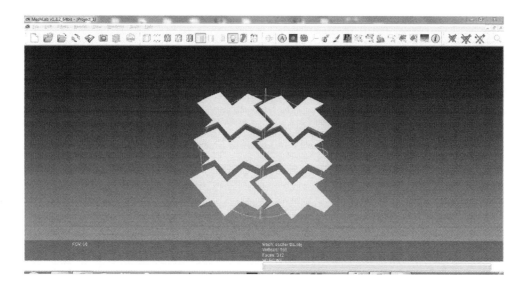

32. From the File menu, choose Export Mesh As... and then save the file as an STL file.

33. You are done! Print several sets of tiles in different colors and see what nice patterns you can make.

Things to do and notice

- This has been a lengthy project because we wanted to showcase some of SketchUp's powerful tools. What other tools could you use to do this project?

- How can you design shapes that look like recognizable animals?

- This project used straight lines for our modified rectangle. Will circular arcs work just as well?

- Instead of rectangles, how can you make Escher-like tiles using triangles or hexagons? (Search for Tessellations online to see lots of resources on this topic.)

15 – Making a Box for Electronic Projects

Design and build a custom box you can use for small electronics projects.

Background

While our focus in this book has been on 3D printing, there are lots of great projects that can combine 3D printing with electrical circuits housing everything from some flashing lights, to a small personal computer, or even to hold the electronics used in a robotics project.

NGSS Areas

Disciplinary Core Idea(s):

- Engineering

How Scientists and Engineers Work:

- Tinkering and experimentation

CCSS Math Connections

- Make sense of problems and persevere in solving them.
- Use appropriate tools strategically.
- Attend to precision.
- Look for and make use of structure.

Materials

- Assorted flashing LEDs
- 3V Lithium batteries (2032) to power the LEDs
- Coin cell battery holders for 2032 batteries
- Miniature toggle switch (single pole, double throw). (All of the items above can be purchased cheaply in bulk from Amazon. You can also probably find them at your local Radio Shack store.)
- 24 ga. insulated wire
- Soldering iron and solder
- A pair of calipers for measuring the diameter of the switch and the LEDs
- Glue gun

Construction details

1. Open Inkscape and draw a square 80 mm on a side.

2. Fill the square with a color of your choice.

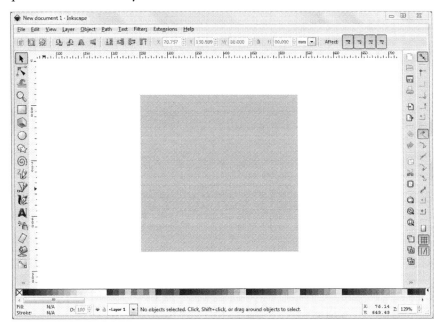

3. Copy this square then paste it in an empty space.

4. Make another filled square with a different color, but make this one 75 mm on a side.

5. Center this square over one of the two 80 mm squares.

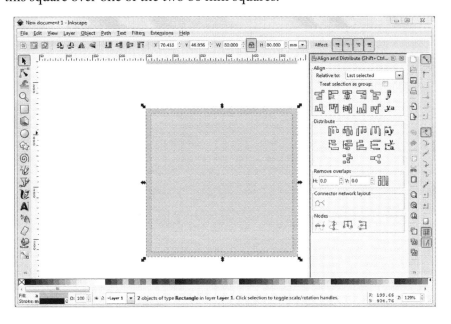

6. Using the Difference tool in the Paths menu, your two squares will turn into a square wall 2.5 mm thick.

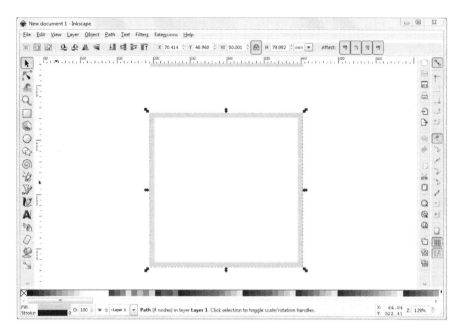

7. For our project, we will put a switch and some flashing lights on the box so it does something when we've finished it. You can, of course, do anything with your box you wish.

8. We need to put some holes in the surface of the box through which the LED lights can shine and where we can mount the switch.

9. Using the calipers, measure the diameter of the plastic shell of the LED just above the base. This will let us push the LED into a hole, without it going all the way through.

10. Repeat this process for the toggle switch. It will be held in place from the front with the hex nut provided with the switch.

11. Using the measurements you just made, make a filled circle with the diameter of the LED, and another with the diameter of the switch bushing.

12. Color these holes with a contrasting color.

13. Place the switch circle at the location on the square platform where you want the switch to be.

14. Paste copies of the LED circle on the platform – for example, three or four.

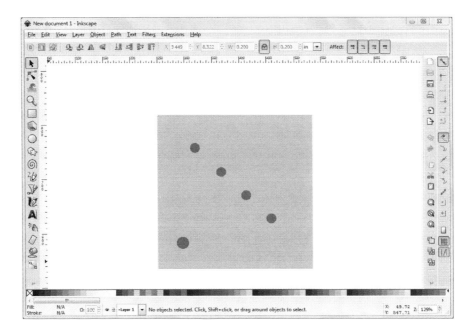

15. Select the square platform and one of the holes.

16. Use the Difference tool in the Paths menu to make your circle a hole.

17. Repeat this process for each of the remaining circles.

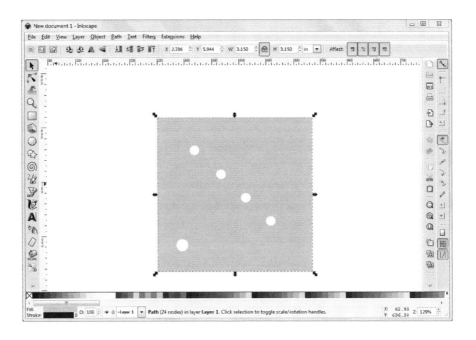

18. Next, select the platform. The current view is the one you would see from the top. But, because of how we will build it, we need to flip it upside down using either the horizontal or vertical flipping tool in Inkscape.

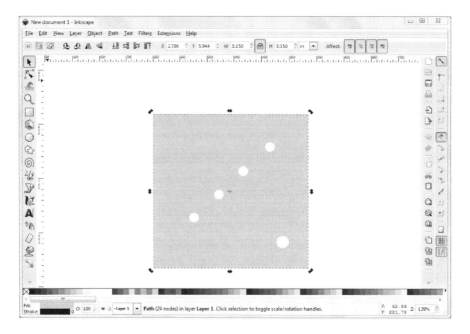

19. It is time to extrude the parts into shapes your 3D printer can make. To do this, select the flipped platform and, from the Extensions menu, choose Generate from Path, and Paths to OpenSCAD. If everything works, you will see a window open that will let you add thickness to your part. Choose the thickness you want – 2.5mm, for example, and then choose an output file name such as [~/desktop/box platform.scad] and click Apply, and then Done. This will generate a file you can open in OpenSCAD.

20. Next, choose the wall outline and repeat this process. In this case, you will want to extrude by 50 mm or so to give you room to put all the electronics inside with nothing sticking out of the bottom. Save this file under another name such as [~/desktop/box platform.scad] and you are ready to assemble your box.

21. But first, save your work!

22. Open each of the OpenSCAD files you just created. Go to the Design menu and choose Compile and Render (F6). Your finished shapes will now show up as 3D objects you can rotate with your mouse to examine from different angles

23. Now go to the Design menu for each shape and choose Export as STL, and save the file on your desktop where it is easy to find: [platform.stl], or [walls.stl], for example.

24. The assembly process is done with Meshlab. Start by importing the platform and wall STL files into Meshlab. If everything goes according to plan, your parts will be aligned into a box that is open at the bottom.

25. Rotate the box to see that it is all properly aligned.

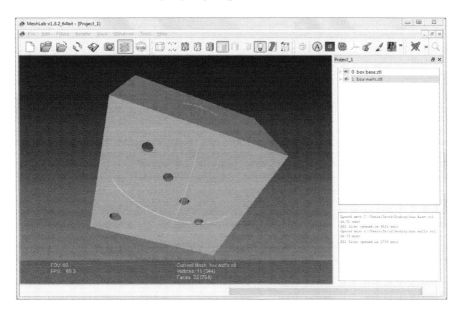

26. Next, click on the layers button (the one that looks like a stack of paper). This opens a window at the right showing both layers of the object.

27. Right-click your mouse on one of the layer names in this window and choose Flatten Image. This puts both pieces together!

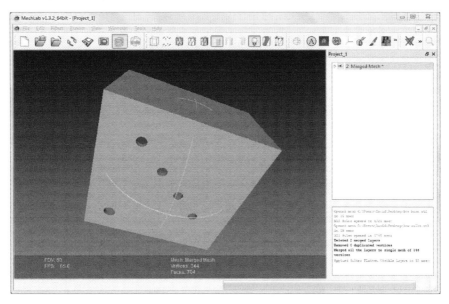

28. Using the Export Mesh command (the icon that looks like a floppy disk), export your finished box as an STL file with a name like [finished box.stl], for example.

29. Print your finished box!

30. The next step is to connect your electronics. That goes a bit beyond the scope of this book, but it quite easy to do and there is lots of supporting information on the Internet. The main thing to remember about LEDs is that they only light up if they are connected the right way. If your lamps don't light up, try reversing the connections and everything should work.

31. One tip on electronics installation: because the box is pretty small, you might want to solder everything together and make sure it works before putting it in the box. Then, put in all the electronics and stick loose pieces like the battery holders to the walls with the glue gun.

Things to do and notice

- This project was just a demonstration (although building a box with flashing LEDs is pretty cool!). If you have a Raspberry Pi computer board, or an Arduino controller board, you can build custom cases for these. In both cases, you need to measure the size of the holes you will need for the USB port, etc.

- Boxes don't have to be rectangular. The same process can be used to make boxes of any shape. For example, design a box with a triangular platform.

16 – Towers of Hanoi

Design and build the Towers of Hanoi puzzle and explore variations of it.

Background

The Towers of Hanoi (also called the Tower of Brahma or Lucas' Tower), is a mathematical puzzle. It consists of three rods, and a number of disks of different sizes which can slide onto any rod. The puzzle starts with the disks in a neat stack in descending order of size on one rod, the smallest at the top, thus making a conical shape.

The objective of the puzzle is to move the entire stack to another rod, obeying the following simple rules:

    1. Only one disk can be moved at a time.

2. Each move consists of taking the upper disk from one of the stacks and placing it on top of another stack i.e., a disk can only be moved if it is the uppermost disk on a stack.

3. No disk may be placed on top of a smaller disk.

The mathematics behind this puzzle is quite interesting and counterintuitive, which probably explains why this puzzle has been popular since it was introduced in 1883 by the mathematician Édouard Lucas, whose pioneering work in the field of prime numbers, among other topics, is well worth exploring on its own.

NGSS Areas

Disciplinary Core Idea(s):

- Engineering

How Scientists and Engineers Work:

- Tinkering and experimentation

CCSS Math Connections

- Make sense of problems and persevere in solving them.
- Reason abstractly and quantitatively.
- Construct viable arguments and critique the reasoning of others.
- Model with mathematics.
- Use appropriate tools strategically.
- Attend to precision.
- Look for and make use of structure.
- Look for and express regularity in repeated reasoning.

Construction details

1. Open Inkscape and draw a circle 60 mm in diameter. Make two copies of this circle and place them in the pattern shown below. If you wish, you can use the Align tool so the two bottom circles are horizontal and just touching. The top circle can then easily be placed by hand.

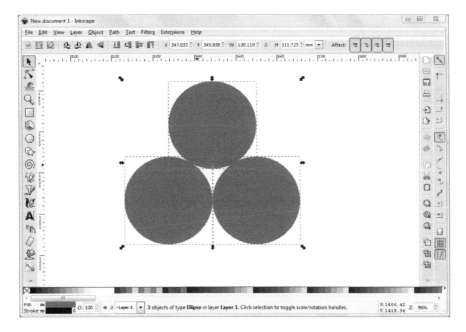

2. Next, make three circles 10 mm in diameter and place them over the centers of the three large circles. You can use the alignment tool if you need to make sure they are exactly centered on each of the circles. These circles will be the basis for the rods, or pillars, of our towers.

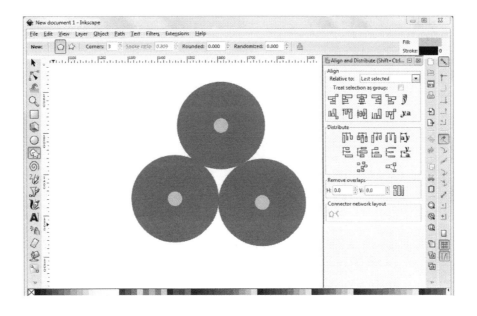

3. Using the polygon tool on the left side toolbar, draw a triangle and size it so the corners pass through the approximate centers of the three small circles.

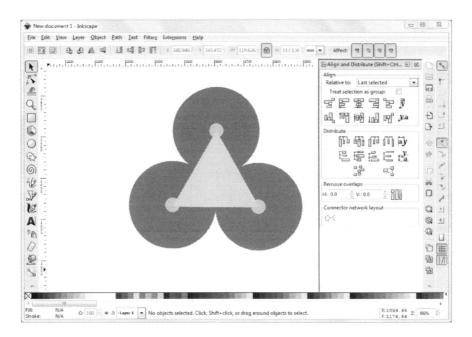

4. Select the small circles and group them (Ctrl G). Move them to the side of the large circles.

5. Select the triangle and three large circles and choose Union from the Path menu. This creates the shape for the base of your towers.

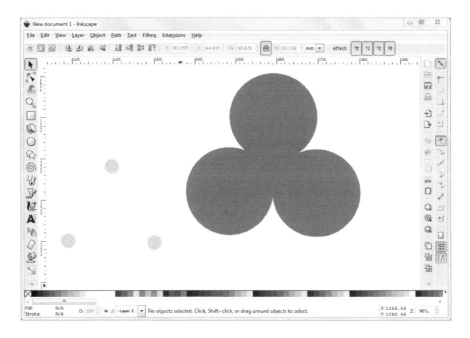

6. Save your work (e.g., [towers.svg]).

7. It is time to extrude the parts into shapes your 3D printer can make. To do this, first select the large part and from the Extensions menu, choose Generate from Path, and Paths to OpenSCAD. If everything works, you will see a window open that will let you add thickness to your part. Choose the thickness you want – 3 mm, for example – and then choose an output file name such as [~/desktop/towerbase.scad] and click Apply, and then Done. This will generate a file you can open in OpenSCAD.

8. Open the OpenSCAD file you just created. Go to the Design menu and choose Compile and Render (F6). Your finished shapes will now show up as a 3D objects you can rotate with your mouse to examine from different angles.

9. Now go to the Design menu and choose Export as STL, and save the file on your desktop where it is easy to find, [towerbase.stl], for example.

10. Repeat this process with the grouped small circles. These will become the pillars of the design and they will export as a group. Extrude these pillars to 50 mm since they have to hold our disks.

11. Save this STL file from OpenSCAD as [~/desktop/towerpillars.scad], for example.

12. The assembly process is done with Meshlab. Start by importing the platform and wall STL files into Meshlab. If everything goes according to plan, your parts will be aligned into a base with three rods sticking out perfectly.

13. Next, click on the layers button (the one that looks like a stack of paper). This opens a window at the right showing both layers of the object.

14. Right-click your mouse on one of the layer names in this window and choose Flatten Image. This puts both pieces together.

15. Using the Export Mesh command (the icon that looks like a floppy disk), export your finished puzzle base as an STL file with a name like [finished puzzlebase.stl], for example.

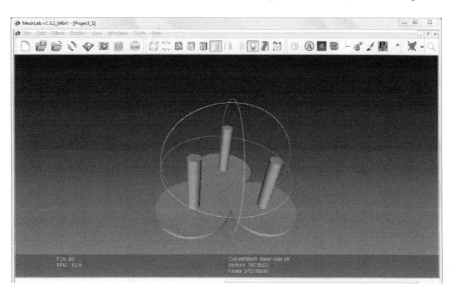

16. Print the base of your puzzle on your 3D printer.

17. Next we need to make some disks to complete our puzzle.

18. Let's start with five disks. Using Inkscape, draw five circles of different sizes: 50 mm, 45 mm, 40 mm, 35 mm, and 30 mm. You can arrange them closely so they all can be printed at once.

19. Since our pillars at 10 mm in diameter, our holes should be a little bigger. Make a circle (with a different fill color) 11 mm in diameter.

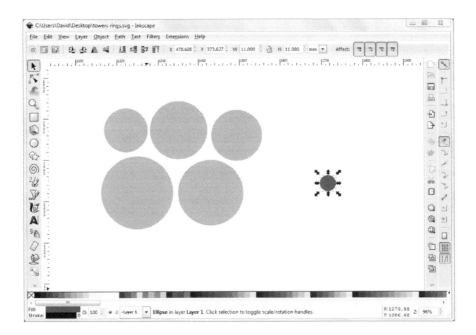

20. Make copies of this small circle and place each copy over the exact center of one of the larger disks. The Align tool should be used for this purpose.

21. Next, select each disk and its center, one pair at a time, and create the hole using the Difference entry in the Path menu.

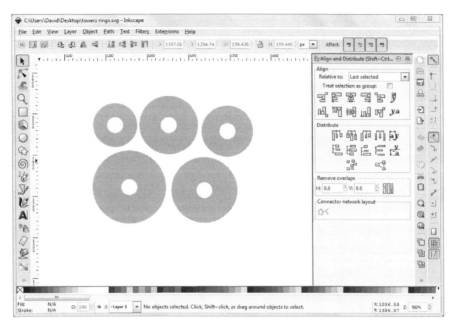

22. Select all five disks and export them to OpenSCAD with an extrusion thickness of 3 mm or so (your choice).

23. With OpenSCAD compile and render the disks and export them to an STL file ([disks.stl], for example).

24. If you wish, look at the completed file in Meshlab, which also cleans the file up a bit.

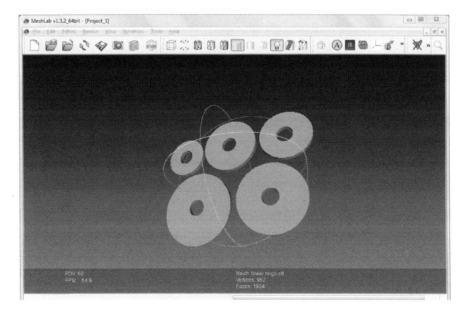

25. Print your disks in a different color than the one you used for your tower.

26. Stack your disks (from largest to smallest) on the left-most rod of your completed base and start working with the puzzle.

Things to do and notice

- If you start with only one disk, it only takes one move to complete the puzzle. With two disks it takes three moves. Find the number of moves needed for different numbers of disks. Can you discern a pattern?

- Were you surprised by the rate at which the number of moves increased for each disk added to the puzzle? If so, what makes the result so counterintuitive?

- Build a new platform in which you add one more rod. What happens to the number of needed moves then? You might want to add a few more disks to the puzzle, each larger than the previous one, to see if you can find a new pattern to the result.

- Next, based on what you've found so far, can you find a relationship between the number of moves for an arbitrary number of disks and rods? For example, if the number of rods equals the number of disks, you will get one result, for different numbers of rods with the same number of disks the results will be different.

17 – Making a Greek Temple

Design and build a model of a temple that might have been used in ancient Greece.

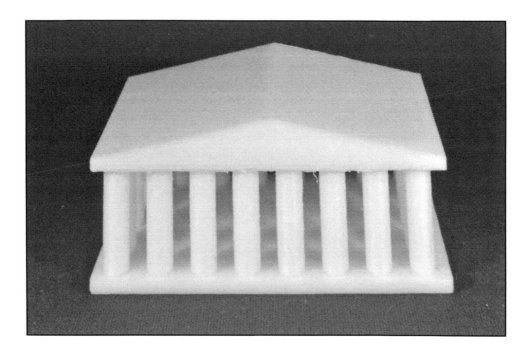

Background

Greek temples like the Parthenon are as beautiful to us today as they were when they were built. This project lets you make a model of a temple to understand its basic parts and construction.

NGSS Areas

Disciplinary Core Idea(s):

- Engineering

How Scientists and Engineers Work:

- Tinkering and experimentation

CCSS Math Connections

- Make sense of problems and persevere in solving them.
- Reason abstractly and quantitatively.
- Use appropriate tools strategically.
- Attend to precision.
- Look for and make use of structure.
- Look for and express regularity in repeated reasoning.

Construction details

1. Launch SketchUp using the 3D Printing millimeters template.
2. Select and delete the Makerbot Replicator2x box.
3. Draw a rectangle with a width of 80 mm and an aspect ratio of the Golden Mean. As you move your mouse, you will see this ratio pop up on the screen when you reach it.
4. With the magnifying glass, zoom into the image so it covers a good area of the screen.

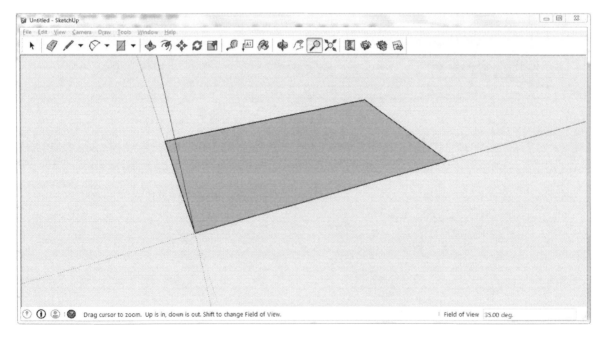

5. Using the Push/Pull tool, drag the bottom of the rectangle down to make a solid plate with a thickness of 3 mm. This is the base of the temple.

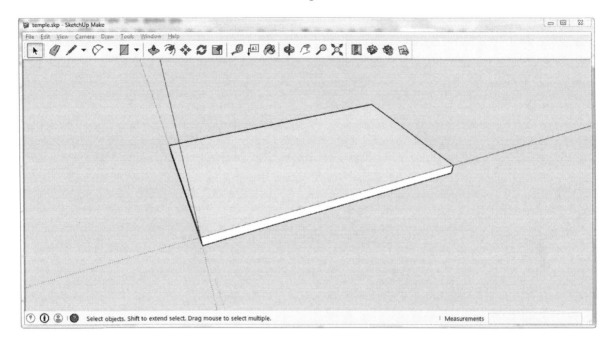

6. Select everything, choose the Move tool (the one with 4 arrows) and click on the front left corner of the base. Holding the Ctrl key down (to make a copy), drag the mouse up to create the base of the roof. Don't worry about how high to go – we will adjust that later.

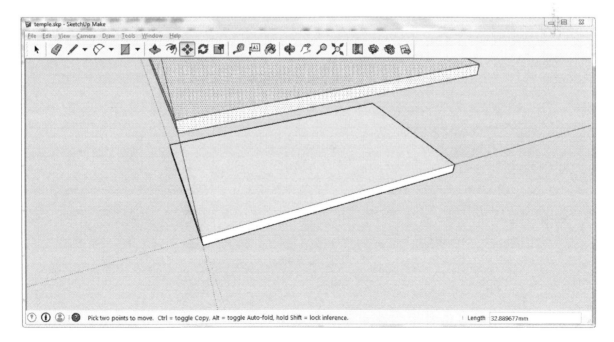

7. Using the Pan tool (shaped like a hand) move the view so the base of the roof is completely visible.

8. Use the pencil tool to draw a line across the top of the roof base from one midpoint to the other. Note that the midpoint will show up when you reach it.

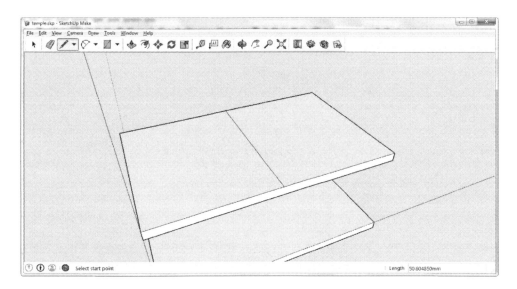

9. Select the midpoint line with the black arrow tool, and pull it up a bit with the Move tool. Move straight up so the roof sides are centered. As you move the line, you will see that it snaps to the right position when you get close. Click the mouse to finish.

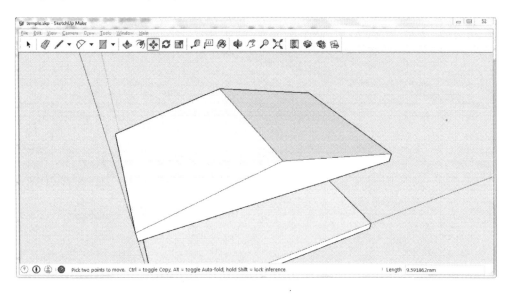

10. Set the Camera view to Front and turn off perspective. Select the entire roof and with the move tool, drag the roof away from the base.

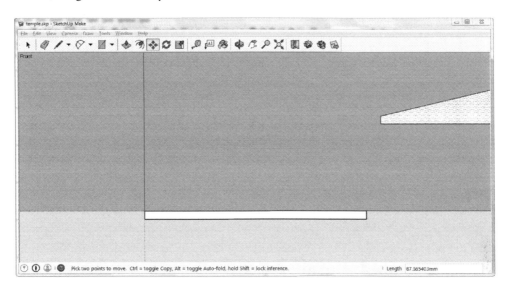

11. Next change the camera view to Iso and draw a circle on the base with a diameter of 3 mm.

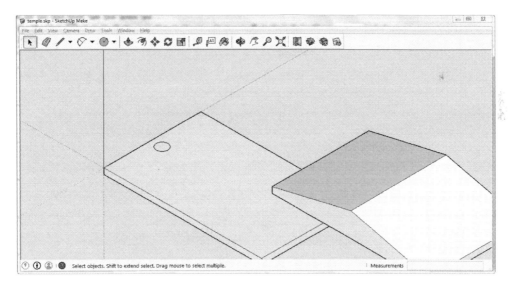

12. Select the circle, and with the Push/Pull tool, pull it into a cylinder 25 mm high. Don't worry abut the position of the column yet.

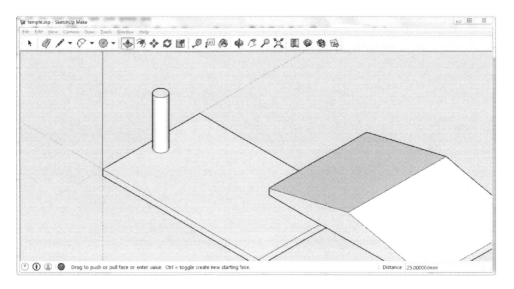

13. Save your work frequently!

14. Next, set the camera to the Top view, select the column and move it to one corner of the temple with the Move tool.

15. With the column still selected, hold down the Ctrl key and move several copies to the edges of the temple as roof supports. For example, move one copy 10 mm and then type 7x to create the rest of the copies along the front of the temple.

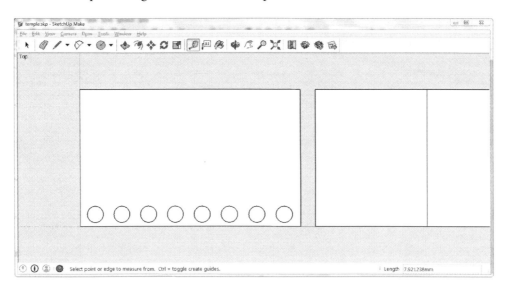

16. Copy these columns and using the Ctrl key and the Move button, place copies at the back edge of the temple.

17. Next, select the top left column and move copies of it along the left edge to finish that side.

18. Finally, select the three interior columns on the left side and Ctrl Move them to the right side. This gives us all the columns, but the alignment might be off – something the ancient Greeks would not have tolerated. Carefully move the columns on each side so they align properly.

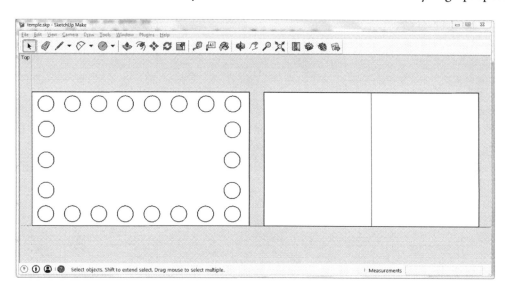

19. Now we are ready to put the roof on our temple. To do this, set the camera to the Front view, select the entire roof and use the Move tool to place it over the columns so the base of the roof is just touching the tops of the columns. Check the other camera views to be sure everything is aligned.

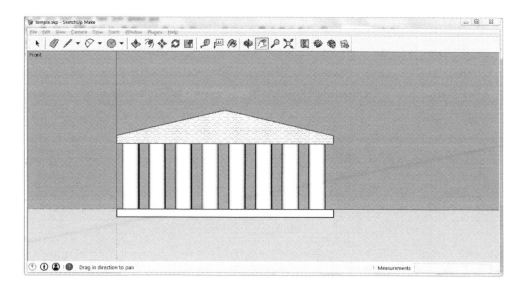

20. Switch to the Iso camera view to see your finished temple design.

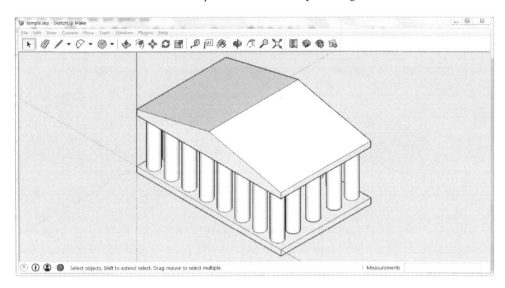

21. Export your 3D model as an OBJ file that you can then load into Meshlab and export as an STL file ready to print!

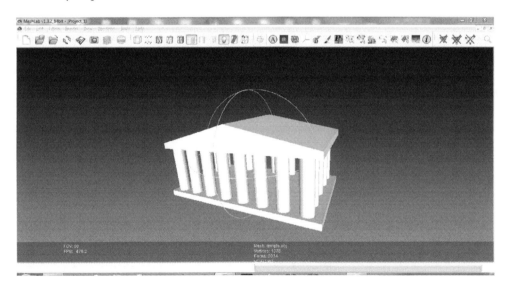

Things to do and notice

- Our temple base has the width and depth based on the Golden Mean or Golden Ratio. Why was this ratio important to the ancient Greeks?

- How many columns are needed to hold a roof properly?

- What role does the diameter of a column have on its strength?

- Greek columns had decorations on the top and bottom. Do some research to find out why these decorations were used.

18 – Designing Your Own Pottery

Design and build your own ceramic pots.

Background

This project breaks two rules we've adopted in this book until now. First, the software isn't free, and second, it doesn't use the classroom printer. So why do it?

Pottery is a craft known since the dawn of humanity – both for function as well as for art. The software we will explore in this project, Let's Create! Pottery (www.potterygame.com), brings the world of pottery to 3D printing. This program exists for iPhones, iPads, Android devices, and the Macintosh computer. Depending on the platform, the price ranges from roughly $5 to$10.

Unlike the traditional 3D modeling software we've explored, this program is set up like a game where you are challenged to design pots or vases of a certain shape and then "fire" and "sell" them in the virtual marketplace. The virtual money you make from sales allows you to purchase everything from colors to patterns and ornaments for your creations.

Once you have a creation ready to be printed, you can place the order through the portal on the program and your pot will be built with a 3D printer that uses ceramic material and sent to you. Depending on the complexity and size of your creation, the price can go as high as about $100. Smaller sizes cost significantly less, so you need to think this all through before placing your order.

The Macintosh version of the software is the hardest to use since you can't use two fingers to "pinch" the boundaries of the clay as it turns on the wheel. In this regard, the iPad and Android tablet versions are probably the best. You have a large screen to look at, and you can use both hands to shape your pot, much as you would with real clay.

NGSS Areas

- N/A

CCSS Math Connections

- N/A

On Your Own

Where To Get Project Ideas

This book has provided you with a wide spectrum of design projects perfect for getting to know the educational potential of your 3D printer. We explored several powerful software titles, and even showed how a construction activity can be extended.

And now, dear reader (and fellow maker), it is time for you to design and build your own projects. Even with this book, it may seem like a daunting task. But don't wait until you have it all figured out and have perfect lesson plans. The best approach is to get started and learn alongside your students. Not only will you see learning through their eyes, they will see you modeling how to learn in a new way, a "maker" way, by jumping in and trying new things. It's good for you and good for them.

Where to get project ideas

Our recommendation is that you keep your eyes open for the kinds of things that are just begging to be made on 3D printers. You may find that the students with whom you work have some great ideas of their own – some more ambitious than others. We think that hard projects are the best ones to do because they fully engage the makers in your class. While the actual printing is time consuming, the design of 3D parts (as you have seen) just involves the use of software – all of it free – that can reside on pretty much any computer in your room. As students work on their own designs, they can benefit from the insights of their peers. In fact, one student may design a part that can be shared for use in other projects – your own local version of Thingiverse!

Above all, you do not need to be responsible for all project ideas. In middle and high school, assign a student or two to track new developments in the 3D world – a 21st Century version of current events! Assign others to watch for new models and designs on websites like Thingiverse. Have a class meeting once a month for students to discuss these new discoveries. Keep lists of potential projects that students can add to or choose from when inspiration strikes.

Most of the 3D project websites listed in the resources have search capability. Search for things like "math" and you will find a whole host of math manipulatives, puzzles, polyhedral, and more. Search for "greek" and you will find greek temples, greek alphabets, etc. You don't have to give students the STL files you find online, but seeing things other people have designed will give you clues to what kinds of things can be 3D printed.

Your students will also soon find that they can download STL files and just print them. Try to discourage this practice by creating more meaningful challenges that require thoughtful, unique designs that are not downloadable. It's fine to get ideas and inspiration from others, but just copying designs will not develop the skills and habits of mind that are possible in this new medium.

Above all, enjoy yourself as you and your students design and build real parts that can be shared with the world at large.

Project starters

When designing your own projects, there is a sequence you and your students should follow.

1. Choose the project
2. Determine which software is best to design your project
3. Do the design
4. Build the project

One advantage of the approach taken in this book is that you and your students have lots of software tools from which to choose. Some of these tools are better suited for some projects than others.

Here are a few ideas to challenge your students – but let their imagination be the driving factor. All of these ideas can be made more challenging by adding constraints or requiring more precision. Extend the learning opportunities by using the creations in other lessons or projects. We've grouped these projects by subject area – and this is just the tip of the iceberg!

Math

- Make a set of Penrose tiles.
- Build a Bean Machine (also known as Galton box). Use plastic B-Bs as the balls.
- Make items that show use of ratio, measurement, scaling, or geometry. Don't forget that scaling doesn't only mean making big things smaller; you can also make small things bigger.

Physics

- Build a balance scale.
- Construct a trebuchet (but be careful where you fire it in the classroom!).
- Make a musical instrument.
- Build simple machines.

Life Sciences

- Make models of simple molecules.
- Construct a model of a DNA fragment.
- Make replica skeletons of body parts (feet, hands, etc.). You can use publicly available X-rays of hands and feet to see the size and placement of the bones.
- Explore the use of 3D printing for medical uses. What do you predict will become common-place in the next few years? Design and print a model of a medical appliance, prosthetic, body part, etc. Defend your choice as being the most likely to change the world.

Earth and Space Sciences

- Design and build rockets that can be launched with compressed air.
- Build a model of the Earth with correct topological features.

Engineering

- Make a model of steam engine.
- Explore the design and construction of watch escapements and Geneva gears.
- Build a functioning clock with minute and hour hands.
- Make an improvement to an everyday household object.
- Bling out your makerspace: wall mounts, tool holders, spacers, drawer labels.
- Design cars and boats and measure speed, launch height, acceleration, etc. Then make them faster, more reliable, and better. Is faster always better?
- Replace missing or broken parts – cranks, knobs, cases, latches, holders, and stands.
- Build a 3D printed bridge. Test and make better. (For an extra challenge, require it to span an opening larger than the largest possible print size.)
- Investigate ancient tools and instruments and make a working model of one.

Language Arts

- Design and make dioramas of scenes from literature (e.g., To Kill a Mockingbird).

Miscellaneous

- Design a toy, statue, bracelet, game piece, dice, action figure, robot, small statue, pencil topper, etc.
- Furnish your dollhouse.
- Create characters or props for a stop-motion video.
- Build sculptures to which you can add light or motion.
- Design a model of your house, classroom, school, or local building.
- Imagine what fossils of modern day plants or animals will look like.
- Make a missing piece for a building set (LEGO, K'Nex, etc.)
- Make a mysterious artifact from another time.
- Design small decorative items and gifts – names in 3D, desk accessories, plaques, bottle openers, keychain fobs, cell phone cases, ear bud holders, luggage tags, beads, and medallions for making jewelry.
- Make a mini-museum full of 3D printed curiosities.
- Invent a three-dimensional symbol that conveys luck, empathy, respect, distress, sadness, etc.
- Design a monument for a nearby park commemorating an event from local history.
- Make props and accessories for the actors in a school play.
- Build an amusement park, zoo, aquarium, or wild animal park.

Resources

Free Software

Tool	Use	URL
Inkscape	2D Illustration software	inkscape.org
Paths2OpenSCAD	3D plugin for Inkscape	Download 'Inkscape to open-SCAD converter v5' from thingiverse.com/thing:25036
OpenSCAD	3D modeling tool with its own language	openscad.org
Meshlab	Clean up and merge 3D files	meshlab.sourceforge.net
3Dtin	3D drawing tool	3dtin.com
123D Design	3D drawing tool	123dapp.com
Meshmixer	3D sculpting tool	meshmixer.com
Sculptris	3D sculpting tool	pixologic.com/sculptris
KnotPlot	3D Knot drawing tool	knotplot.com
SketchUp Make	3D drawing tool	sketchup.com
Tinkercad	3D drawing tool	tinkercad.com

3D Printer Designs and Community Sites

Site	Use	URL
Thingiverse	STL file repository. Sponsored by Makerbot, but files can be used in any printer.	thingiverse.com
YouMagine	Online community for 3D printing	youmagine.com
SketchUp Warehouse	3D image repository	3dwarehouse.sketchup.com
Instructables	A variety of projects using 3D printers and objects	instructables.com/tag/type-id/category-technology/channel-3D-Printing

| Make Magazine | 3D printing projects and printer reviews | makezine.com/category/ workshop/3d-printing-workshop |
| AutoDesk | 3D models for Autodesk apps | 123dapp.com/Gallery |

Outsourced Printing and Plating

Site	Use	URL
RePliKote	Plate plastic models with metal	repliforminc.com/RePliKote.htm
Shapeways	Makes 3D models from your art in variety of materials.	shapeways.com
Ponoko	3D print, laser cut, and sell your designs	ponoko.com
Sculpteo	3D print your own designs, buy and sell 3D printed objects	sculpteo.com

Glossary

ABS – Acrylonitrile butadiene styrene. This is a type of plastic used as filaments in many 3D printers. It is recyclable. The downside is that it shrinks a bit on cooling, so the platform on the printer should be heated to about 100 C. Finished parts are stronger and less brittle than those made with PLA.

Build plate – A removable, reusable surface on which the 3D object is extruded.

CAD, Computer Aided Design – Refers to the steps taken to build a 3D product to be printed.

CCSS, Common Core State Standards – These are new sets of standards for K–12 education that focus on mathematics and language arts. The math standards are designed to help students to learn to think like mathematicians, and aspects of these standards are explored in most of the projects in this book.

Extrusion – The process by which a heated plastic filament is pushed through a nozzle. The temperature at which extrusion is possible is in the range of 250 C, so the extrusion nozzle gets quite hot. The process of extrusion allows building a 3D object from a 2D design.

NGSS, Next Generation Science Standards – This new set of K–12 standards applies to the sciences and engineering (which is now a core part of the K–12 curriculum in states adopting these standards). They were developed over a period of years to transform education in these subjects. Many of the projects in this book are connected to these standards, especially the engineering component.

OBJ – One format for 3D drawings – not generally preferred for 3D printing. If you have a drawing saved in the OBJ format, it can be converted to STL through use of the Meshlab program.

Parametric designs – These are designs that can be modified by changing a few parameters to get the exact shape you want. For example, a parametric design for a propeller might let you choose the radius, blade width, and number of blades. 3D designs written in the native language for OpenSCAD are often created this way to maximize their value.

PLA, Polyactic Acid – This is one of two plastics used as filaments in many 3D printers. It is extracted from Cassava roots, comes in many colors, and is (slowly) biodegradable. It has minimal shrinkage. The downside is that it is not as strong as ABS.

Raft – A rectangular piece of material that sits on the plate on which your object will be extruded. It helps prevent warping, and makes the printed piece more stable as it is being printed. You will peel the raft off of your printed piece and throw it away after printing.

SCAD – A format for 3D designs that consists of a text file in a special programming language that describes every element of the design. This is very useful for the creation of parametric designs.

STL files – STL stands for Standard Tessellation Language or Stereo Lithography, and is the format the printer understands in order to print your object.

Support material – When you print your object, it may need support as it is being printed, so thin pieces of material will build out to provide that support. You will carefully break off the extra material after printing, leaving only your object.

SVG – Scalable vector graphics format used for two-dimensional drawings. It has many great features including the ability to be scaled to any size without losing sharpness of the original drawing. This is the native format used by Inkscape. When the right extension is installed, Inkscape can export a flat drawing as an extrusion for use in constructing 3D parts.

Tensegrity – A word coined by renowned architect Buckminster Fuller, tensegrity is a structural principle based on the use of isolated components in compression inside a net of continuous tension.

About the Authors

David Thornburg, PhD: David@knights-of-knowledge.com

Through presentations, workshops and books, Dr. David Thornburg uses his expertise in emerging trends to help educators build the skills needed to use technology as a tool to teach for understanding, backed by solid research and a coherent vision of an educational future in which every learner thrives. A staunch advocate of STEM education, he sees 3D printing as a powerful tool in the hands of all students.

Norma Thornburg, MA: Norma@knights-of-knowledge.com

Norma Thornburg is an exceptional educator. Using her knowledge of emerging trends in technology, she helps teachers develop constructivist strategies to engage students in learning activities that build valuable life skills for the 21st Century. Her interest in making covers a wide range. She has taught robotics courses, and is now working in the area of "soft circuits" – fabric creations with embedded circuitry – and in the crafting of ceramics using specialized 3D printers.

Sara Armstrong, PhD: Sara@knights-of-knowledge.com

Dr. Sara Armstrong is an educational consultant, keynote speaker, presenter, and writer working to provide resources and tools for change in education. With over 40 years as an educator, Sara has developed and implemented workshops on many topics, including project-based learning, information literacy, digital and oral tradition storytelling, technology integration, and global resources for education. She sees 3D printing as a powerful tool for bringing inquiry and project-based learning into the classroom.

Also from Constructing Modern Knowledge Press

Invent To Learn: Making, Tinkering, and Engineering in the Classroom

by Sylvia Libow Martinez and Gary Stager

There's a technological and creative revolution underway. Amazing new tools, materials and skills turn us all into makers. Using technology to make, repair or customize the things we need brings engineering, design and computer science to the masses. Fortunately for educators, this maker movement overlaps with the natural inclinations of children and the power of learning by doing. The active learner is at the center of the learning process, amplifying the best traditions of progressive education.

In this practical guide, Sylvia Martinez and Gary Stager provide K–12 educators with the how, why, and cool stuff that supports classroom making.

Available in print and e-book version at InventToLearn.com

"Learning is often confused with education. Martinez and Stager clearly describe 'learning learning' through engagement, design and building. The best way to understand circles is to reinvent the wheel." — *Nicholas Negroponte, Founder MIT Media Lab & One Laptop Per Child*

"The Maker Movement in schools now has a bible." — *Larry Magid, Technology Columnist, Huffington Post, San Jose Mercury News, CBS Radio*

"Educators will be hard pressed to find a more essential, important book for making sense of not just the exciting, game-changing "maker" technologies that are currently exploding around us, but of the absolutely powerful learning opportunities they present for our students as well. Sylvia Martinez and Gary Stager are a teacher's perfect guides into this fast growing, innovative world of creative problem solving and construction using an array of new, innovative computing devices, many of which fit in our pockets. Even more, Invent To Learn creates a required new context for modern learning, and it offers an accessible roadmap for re-imagining schools, classrooms, and personal practice. It's a must read for those wanting to remain relevant in their student's learning lives." — *Will Richardson, Author of Why School? How Education Must Change When Learning and Information Are Everywhere*

Made in the USA
Lexington, KY
18 September 2014